EDWIN ALONZO BOYD

AMAZING STORIES

EDWIN ALONZO BOYD

The Life and Crimes of
Canada's Master Bank Robber

HISTORY/BIOGRAPHY

by Nate Hendley

PUBLISHED BY ALTITUDE PUBLISHING CANADA LTD.
1500 Railway Avenue, Canmore, Alberta T1W 1P6
www.altitudepublishing.com
1-800-957-6888

Publisher	Stephen Hutchings
Associate Publisher	Kara Turner
Project Editor	Jill Foran
Editor	Geoff McKenzie
Digital photo coloration	Scott Manktelow

We acknowledge the financial support of the Government
of Canada through the Book Publishing Industry Development
Program (BPIDP) for our publishing activities.

Altitude GreenTree Program
Altitude Publishing will plant twice as many trees as were used
in the manufacturing of this product.

National Library of Canada Cataloguing in Publication Data

Hendley, Nate.
Edwin Alonzo Boyd / Nate Hendley

(Amazing stories)
Includes bibliographical references.
ISBN 1-55153-968-3

1. Boyd, Edwin Alonzo, 1914-2002. Bank robberies--Ontario--Toronto. 3.
Brigands and robbers--Ontario--Toronto--Biography. I. Title. II. Series:
Amazing stories (Canmore, Alta.)
HV6653.B69H46 2003   364.15'52'092   C2003-911125-3

Printed and bound in Canada by Friesens
2 4 6 8 9 7 5 3

Cover: Edwin Alonzo Boyd being arrested in 1952
(*Toronto Star* file photo)

Photographs page 8 and 109 also *Toronto Star* file photos

This book is dedicated to my family,
who was there

TORONTO DAILY STAR

60TH YEAR

SATURDAY, MARCH 15, 1952—48 PAGES

3c PER COPY, 18c PER-WEEK

THE WEATHER
Toronto and vicinity — Sunday:
Sunny; low tonight, 20; high Fri-
day, 35.

HOME AND SPORT EDITION

Trail's end . . . .

60 POLICE NAB SLEEPING BOYD, WIFE SEIZE $25,037, GUNS

Led in Chains From Hideout

JAUNTY BOYD SMILES AFTER CAPTURE

GUN MUZZLE UNDER NOSE BOYD AWAKENS, SURRENDERS SAYS 'YOU DID FINE JOB'

By FRANK TESKEY

The climax of the greatest police manhunt in Canada's crime history was written without a shot today when Edwin Alonzo Boyd, last of a trio of desperate gunmen, looked up from his bed in a Heath St. W. apartment into the muzzle of a police revolver.

Within reach of the twin beds where Boyd slept with his pretty brunette wife was an open briefcase with a fully loaded heavy-calibre pistol and $25,037.81 in cash, but the prisoner made no move to fight. In a coat hanging beside the bed were bags of pepper, ready to throw at pursuers and temporarily blind them.

Taken into custody in the same house on the quiet street, a stone's throw from Yonge St., was Boyd's brother Norman. The wife and brother will both be held, police said. They moved into the house only last night.

Thugs convoyed Boyd to the apartment in three cars, police revealed. While the gang-land escort hustled the wanted man into what they thought was safety, police munched sandwiches from their observation posts, then swung into action.

CAPTURE MATCHES HOLLYWOOD MOVIE SCENE

The capture scene matched any Hollywood movie. Just before dawn an army of 60 police armed with machine-guns, tear gas, rifles and revolvers converged on the house on the north side of the street as Sergt. of Detectives Adolphus Payne and his partner, Det. Ken Craven, slipped silently in by front and back doors.

With guns drawn they poked quickly and quietly into each room in order. Payne pushed open the second room from the front on the second floor, and there, in bed only a few feet away, were Boyd and his wife.

PULL GUN, MONEY OUT OF REACH

The open briefcase beside the bed with the pistol plainly visible was pulled out of reach. Craven moved in to take Boyd's brother, also at gunpoint, and within seconds the house was swarming with armed detectives.

Chief of Police John Chisholm, Deputy Chief Moses Mulholland, Inspector John Nimmo and Inspector Archie McCathie were on the scene to direct precautions against any possible move for a break.

A wide-eyed black tomcat, only occupant of the house awake when detectives came through the door, might have tipped the hand of police, but like an inside man on the job, he never uttered a sound.

Instead, he silently trailed the officers through the house and yawned a big wide-eyed yawn of satisfaction when the prisoner was manacled.

MAYOR SEES CAPTURE COMPLETED

Mayor Lamport sped to the spot and arrived in time to see the capture completed. He congratulated police and saw Boyd and his brother securely manacled.

"I didn't think it would take some thing like this to meet your worship."

(Continued on Page 5, Col. 1)

MANACLED CAPTIVE IS LED AWAY, ON LEFT MAYOR LAMPORT AND SGT. PAYNE

FRANK TESKEY

CHISHOLM, PAYNE, CRAVEN, MULHOLLAND, LAMPORT

STAR PUZZLE CONTEST BEGINS NEXT THURSDAY PRIZES TOTAL $25,000

BEGINS THURSDAY, MARCH 20

Contents

Prologue

Edwin Alonzo Boyd's fingers twitched as he tapped the 7.45 mm automatic pistol tucked in his belt. The weapon was one of five handguns in his possession, all of them loaded and ready for action. A briefcase filled with stolen cash lay on the floor of his bedroom.

It was March 1952. The Korean War was still raging but the public seemed more interested in a newfangled invention called television. Dwight Eisenhower would soon be elected president of the United States, and the Toronto Maple Leafs were one of the hottest teams in the National Hockey League.

But Boyd had no time to think about television or politics or hockey. He had other things to worry about. For a start, scores of policemen were scouring the country for him. As head of the so-called Boyd Gang, he had organized some of the most spectacular bank robberies in Canada's history. His face had been splashed on the front pages of newspapers across the nation, and his gun-slinging exploits had become the stuff of legend.

Edwin Alonzo Boyd

The son of a respected police officer, Boyd was an army veteran with an adoring wife and three kids. He had charm, athletic skills, and loads of charisma. And yet there he was, a wanted man in a rented room, waiting for the police to come crashing through his door.

In years to come, Boyd would have plenty of time to ponder how his life had "gone bad." For now, however, his only concern was keeping out of jail and hanging on to whatever cash remained from his tenure as Canada's number one bank robber.

Chapter 1
Boyd's Beginnings

dwin Boyd moved quickly down Toronto's Danforth Avenue, his small hands pounding against the cement. The boy was busy making deliveries, but instead of walking normally or riding a bicycle, he was shuffling along the sidewalk on his hands. This was the kind of nimble trick that young Boyd loved to perform. Almost a teenager, he was wiry and strong, and possessed the trim physique of a long distance runner. While not walking on his hands, Boyd liked to impress his friends by doing dramatic back flips. He was good-looking, charming, and physically gifted. In essence,

Edwin Alonzo Boyd

he seemed like the ideal Canadian kid.

Edwin Alonzo Boyd was born on April 2, 1914, to a loving mother named Eleanor and a tough, disciplinarian father named Glover. Boyd's father was very religious, and had a no-nonsense attitude towards raising children. Just months after Boyd was born, World War I broke out in Europe. In August of 1915, Glover Boyd joined the Canadian Army and was shipped overseas, where he stayed for the duration of the war. While his father was away, young Boyd became quite close to his mother. He also grew very close to his half-brother Harold, Eleanor's son from a previous relationship.

When Glover returned to Toronto after the war, young Boyd's happy, close-knit family life came to an end. Accustomed to commanding his mother's complete attention, the five-year-old now had to compete with an unfamiliar man for her affections. It was a trying moment in Boyd's early life.

Aside from his father's long absence, Boyd's childhood was relatively uneventful. Like most children, he spent almost all of his free time playing with friends. In the summers Boyd and his pals would often take a streetcar to the Don Valley, a huge ravine that cuts Toronto down the middle. There, they would swim and splash around in the valley's muddy waters.

Throughout the 1920s, the Boyd family went

through a number of changes. In 1920, Eleanor gave birth to a son named Gordon. A third son, Norman, and a daughter, Irene, soon followed. As the family grew, Boyd's father took a job as a policeman on the Toronto police force, where he would go on to spend a quarter-century in uniform.

Due to various mix-ups, Boyd didn't enter school until he was seven years old. Amidst all the turmoil caused by raising a rapidly growing family, his parents forgot to enrol their son in elementary school. Once Eleanor realized their mistake, she quickly placed Boyd in the local school.

As it turned out, "book learning" held little appeal for young Boyd. He didn't care much for the strict discipline and regimentation common to education at the time. Indeed, Boyd was far more interested in athletics than academia. He liked to incorporate his athletic skills into the odd jobs he took after school. It was while delivering meat for a butcher on the Danforth that he started the practice of walking on his hands.

The older Boyd got, the more distant he grew from his father. He didn't like his father's strict rules, or the fact that his dad forced him to learn the violin. But Glover wanted his oldest child to set an example for the rest of the children in the family. When Boyd misbehaved, his father didn't hesitate to swat him with a hockey stick, or any other piece of equipment that happened to be nearby.

Though his relationship with Glover continued to deteriorate, Boyd remained very close with his mother, whose gentle nature had somewhat of a calming effect. Sadly, Eleanor died when Boyd was only 15 — a devastating blow for the teenaged boy. After Eleanor passed away, Glover hired an Irish immigrant named Minerva to help run the household, and as time passed, the policeman fell in love with his housekeeper.

Boyd dropped out of school a year after his mother's death, having only managed to pass grade eight. His lack of scholastic achievement might have been a reflection of his parents' easy-going attitude towards education. In later years, Boyd claimed that his mother and father never bought him books or read to him as a child.

No matter who was to blame for Boyd's dropping out of school, his decision was not an unusual one. In the 1920s and 1930s, it wasn't uncommon for boys and girls to leave school early. Boyd's timing, however, was particularly bad. In 1929, Canada entered the Great Depression. Businesses went bankrupt, farms became dusty wastelands, and factories stopped turning out manufactured goods. Finding work was difficult for anyone, but it was near impossible for an undereducated young man who didn't like following orders.

Boyd's Beginnings

Nonetheless, Boyd was eager to strike out on his own. With his mother gone and his father romancing Minerva, he was no longer comfortable being at home. At the age of 18, he left Toronto and became part of a large group of rootless young men who travelled from city to city on boxcars.

While a lucky handful of men his age were applying themselves in university or college, Boyd received an education of a different sort. Fellow tramps taught him how to hustle for money and beg for a meal. It was like being a salesman in a way: he had to develop a good pitch and learn how to be charming in a hurry. The alternative was to go hungry.

Boyd proved to be a good student. Unlike the lessons that had bored him in school, the lessons he learned on the road had practical applications. For someone who hated formal education, Boyd was remarkably eager to soak up new knowledge, provided it had a practical benefit.

Using techniques he learned from fellow wanderers, Boyd got quite good at swindling and hustling. Caging free meals became one of his most common scams. Typically, Boyd and a companion would clean their clothes as best they could, then enter a restaurant. They would sit at a table and order a big meal, as if money were no object. Once the meal was eaten and the waiter was preparing the check, Boyd and his companion would announce that they had no money but that they would be happy to wash dishes or provide some other form of menial labour to pay off their tab. In most cases, the restaurant managers agreed to this offer, usually to save themselves the aggravation of having to call the police and file a complaint. Besides, even the snootiest restaurant manager knew that thousands of young men were out of work.

But Depression or not, Boyd was a natural charmer who was good at getting people to give him what he wanted. This dubious talent was no doubt aided by the fact that the young man was movie star handsome. With his slender build, shiny black hair, and piercing eyes, Boyd closely resembled matinee idol Errol Flynn. Such a resemblance was sure to help Boyd charm even the most tight-fisted of targets.

Unfortunately for Boyd, his charm wasn't always enough to keep him out of trouble with the law. In November of 1933, he and a friend were arrested for vagrancy, which was then a criminal offence. Both men were fined $20 — a lot of money in the 1930s, especially for an unemployed young man. Boyd couldn't pay the fine and consequently he had to serve six weeks in jail. He did his time at Fort Saskatchewan prison, near Edmonton, Alberta.

Boyd's Beginnings

In January of 1934, after serving his time in jail, Boyd entered a relief camp near Calgary. The camp was one of several run by the federal government, and its purpose was to provide young men with food, shelter, and a little money in exchange for putting in long hours of hard work. Some of the undesirable jobs available in these camps included clearing brush, moving rocks, and digging holes. Among other chores, Boyd helped construct part of the Trans-Canada Highway.

Not surprisingly, Boyd didn't last long in the labour camp. After only a few weeks he could no longer tolerate the camp's highly regimented system, so he decided to make his way back to Toronto. Glover assured his son that he was welcome to stay at the family home. But Boyd wasn't convinced that this was the best solution. In the end, the lure of the road proved too strong for him to resist. Once more, Boyd began drifting from city to city, begging for food and money, and committing minor crimes to get by.

In February of 1935, Boyd was arrested for begging in Saskatoon. Once again, he couldn't pay his fine and was consequently thrown in jail. He served two months in Saskatchewan's Moosomin Jail. After his release, Boyd divided his time between living with his father in Toronto and living the life of a hobo. He also began committing more serious crimes, including car theft and other forms of amateur burglary.

In the summer of 1936, while walking around the outskirts of Saskatoon in the middle of the night, Boyd and a companion decided to rob a gas station. The gas station in question was closed and there weren't any houses nearby. After breaking into the building through a window, the two burglars began searching for the cash drawer when a police officer drove by. As it turned out, the constable was on routine patrol. He parked his cruiser and strode to the gas station, flashlight in hand. While making his regular inspection of the building, he discovered the broken window and began to make his way inside the station.

Realizing that the officer was going to enter the building, Boyd hid under a nearby desk. He stayed there for several minutes as the policeman checked out the inside of the gas station, then sat down at the very desk that Boyd was using for cover. The constable lit a cigarette then phoned the gas station manager to inform him about the break-in. Feeling something strange by his feet, the policeman shined his flashlight under the desk and discovered Boyd staring up at him.

Once again, Boyd was arrested. This time, police charged him with the gas station break-in, and with a slew of other crimes as well. Boyd insisted he hadn't taken part in all the offences he was charged with, but it didn't matter. On September 3, 1936, Boyd pled guilty in an Edmonton courtroom and was handed a three-and-a-half year sentence. He was then shipped off to the Saskatchewan Penitentiary, in Prince Albert. Like most inmates, Boyd didn't care much for jail. But he did his best to stay out of trouble with the guards and his fellow prisoners. Boyd knew that if he acted up he would get more time added to his sentence. After serving his three and half years, Boyd was released in March of 1939. At almost 25 years old he had no real job skills — except for the ones he had picked up from fellow tramps and criminals.

Not sure what to do next, Boyd moved back to Toronto. He picked up odd jobs here and there and saved enough money to buy a motorcycle. He soon came to savour the feeling of independence and speed that the motorcycle provided. While out riding, Boyd tried to figure out what to do with his life. Going back to being a hobo didn't seem so attractive now that he was no longer a teenager. Then again, working for minimum wage at a dead-end job wasn't too appealing either.

Boyd rode, worried, and dreamed, never imagining that events in Europe were about to change his life forever.

Chapter 2

World War II

On September 1, 1939, Germany invaded Poland and triggered the start of a new world war. In the days that followed, Canadians sat glued to their radios, listening to the latest broadcasts from overseas. Paperboys hawked the most up-to-date newspapers, all of which were splashed with huge, frightening headlines about the war. Newsreels in movie theatres featured sombre pronouncements by politicians and global leaders. Within days of Hitler's invasion, Great Britain declared war on Germany, and on September 10, 1939, Canada joined the fight.

While World War II was a time of hardship and strife for millions of people, for Edwin Boyd and countless other unemployed Canadians, it proved to be somewhat of a boon. Young men who had spent the Depression jobless and homeless now flocked to join the army. With a war on, the Canadian government spared no expense with its defence forces. Ottawa poured money into the army, which expanded from a tiny force to a huge military organization.

Boyd enlisted in the Canadian Forces in the fall of 1939. Much to his delight, the army didn't care about his criminal past. Boyd's father was delighted, too. He figured his son might finally straighten himself out. And for a while, he did.

Once Boyd finished his basic military training in Quebec, he was shipped overseas to England. It was a dangerous voyage. German submarines called U-boats were prowling the Atlantic Ocean, looking for Allied ships to sink. However, Boyd made it to his destination without incident.

Because of his familiarity with motorcycles, Boyd was made a dispatch rider soon after he arrived in England. His duties allowed him to spend most of the war riding around the English countryside. Though he was supposed to be delivering important messages to his superiors, it seemed he always found time for scenic detours. It was a good life, and a lot less dangerous than serving on the front lines. For all his dislike of authority and routine, Boyd didn't mind being a soldier. The army gave him a sense of direction and purpose. It also provided him with steady pay, free food, clothing, and accommodations. And of course, the fact that Boyd was able to spend most of his time on a motorcycle also shaped his positive attitude towards the military.

In 1940, while carrying out an assignment just south of London, Boyd met Dorreen Mary Thompson, an attractive, dark-haired woman from northern England. Though Dorreen was just 20 years old when she met Boyd, she had already been through some very difficult times. When Dorreen was just a child, her mother had become seriously ill, and her grandparents had taken over the task of raising her. Later, Dorreen's mother and grandmother waged a bitter, hateful battle over her custody. As the battle raged, Dorreen had become more and more unruly, and eventually she was sent to a Catholic convent that housed "delinquent" girls.

Boyd and Dorreen were instantly attracted to each other, and within a short time they were in love. The young couple was married on November 21, 1940. Not too long after the wedding, Dorreen revealed to Boyd that she had a son from a previous relationship. The child's name was Anthony, and he was six months old.

Despite this surprise announcement, Boyd gallantly stood by his new wife, and soon the couple was expecting a baby of their own. Dorreen gave birth to Edwin Alonzo Boyd Jr. in August of 1941. The boy was born in Dorreen's hometown of York, England. Unfortunately for the Boyds, York was one of several cities targeted by the Luftwaffe — the mighty German air force. Two days after Edwin Jr. was born, York was hit by a wave of German bombers. Antiaircraft guns began hurling shells into the sky as air sirens wailed their eerie warnings. Workers in the hospital ward where Edwin Jr. slept rushed frantically to move the tiny infants into a nearby bomb shelter. A nurse scooped Edwin Jr. into her arms and, carrying five other babies at the same time, raced out of the nursery. In her haste, she accidentally hit Edwin Jr.'s head on a doorjamb. The baby suffered massive brain damage and died days later.

Boyd and Dorreen were devastated by the death of their first child. But as if to make up for their loss, Dorreen quickly became pregnant again with twins. In December of 1943 she gave birth to a boy and a girl. As Boyd began to adjust to family life, the war was entering its final, bloody stages.

In early June of 1944, American, British, and Canadian forces landed on the French coast in the dramatic D-Day campaign. By the summer, the Allies had firmly established themselves in France, but at a high cost. The Germans fought tenaciously for every inch of land they gave up. A few weeks after the D-Day landings, Boyd was shipped to France. Though he didn't serve on the frontlines, he witnessed plenty of death and destruction.

Boyd moved through a landscape filled with the debris of war. Shattered tanks and bomb craters dotted the killing fields. Dead Canadian soldiers in their drab brown uniforms lay next to their grey-clad German counterparts. As he walked through the hellish terrain, Boyd spotted something that he wanted to keep as a souvenir. It was a Luger pistol — a common side arm for German troops — and it belonged to a dead Nazi soldier who was lying upside down on the seat of a horse-drawn wagon. Figuring the soldier wouldn't need the pistol anymore, Boyd grabbed the Luger for himself. During his time in the army, Boyd also stole a Thompson sub-machine gun, a lethal weapon favoured by British and American troops.

While Boyd was stationed in France, Dorreen was preparing for a major life change. Shortly before Christmas of 1944, Dorreen and her three children left their home in England and sailed on a troop ship to Canada. After docking in Halifax, Dorreen and the children journeyed to Toronto, where they were met and welcomed by Boyd's father, Glover. By that time, Glover Boyd and Minerva were married and had a nine-year-old son named Howard. Although the older couple didn't have much room for Boyd's wife and children, they invited Doreen to stay with them nonetheless.

In February of 1945, with the war winding down and his family safely lodged at his father's home, Boyd was finally sent back to Canada. The ship that carried Boyd home was filled with returning troops and war brides. Everyone was so elated to be leaving war-torn Europe that no one bothered to take a look at the contents of Boyd's duffle bag. Inside, hidden among a collection of clothing, was the Luger pistol and the stripped-down parts of the Thompson submachine gun. Of course, it was against the rules for soldiers to take home weapons acquired during their terms of duty. But ever the rebel, Boyd chose to ignore those rules.

Though he had returned to Canada heavily armed, Boyd had no immediate intentions of using either of his guns. He was much more interested in getting reunited with his family and adjusting to civilian life. A few weeks after settling in Toronto, Boyd was officially discharged from the military. The war in Europe was clearly won, and the Canadian government figured they no longer needed such a big army.

That spring, Boyd took a job as a streetcar conductor with the Toronto Transit Commission (TTC). It was a good, steady government position that promised decent wages and job security. After landing his new job, Boyd moved his family to a home in northern Toronto. Like millions of other returning military veterans, he was settling down. The former hobo and petty thief was now a municipal employee and a family man, albeit one with two illegal guns and a thirst for action.

Chapter 3
A Career Switch

E dwin Boyd stopped his Toronto streetcar, opened its door, and let on a series
of passengers. He nodded politely as
people boarded the vehicle, then shut the door and
drove away. Even in his crisp, Toronto Transit
Commission uniform, Boyd looked more like a movie
star than a city worker. Many women on his streetcar
cast eyes at him, wondering who he was and if he was
available.

But while the female passengers were pleased with
their handsome young driver, Boyd himself felt restless
in his new life as a TTC employee. Though driving a

streetcar was steady work, it was certainly nowhere near as exhilarating as riding through England on a motorbike. Instead of having to contend with landmines and the bodies of dead soldiers in the fields of France, all Boyd now had to worry about was making his route on time.

Not only was he bored with his job, he was also bored with Toronto itself. Indeed, the complacent ambiance of his hometown was quite a letdown from the buzzing, battle-scarred cities of London and York, England. In the late 1940s, Toronto was a big city with a small-town atmosphere. At that time, the city was home to few minorities, and it exuded a quaint, British air. There weren't many bars and restaurants, and most stores closed on Sundays. But if Toronto was boring, it was also very safe. The crime rate was very low, nothing like that of American cities.

As Boyd drove his streetcar up and down Toronto tracks, he spent a great deal of time pondering his future. He felt destined for bigger things. Surely, a man with his good looks, athletic skills, and charm shouldn't be spending his time driving passengers around Toronto.

In March of 1946, after a year at his job, Boyd quit the TTC. It wasn't a decision that was made or taken lightly. Because he had a criminal record, it would be tough for him to get another job with the transit commission. But Boyd didn't want anything to do with the TTC. Instead, he took up a series of menial jobs, working mostly as a janitor and a night watchman. At one point, he delivered groceries, just like he had as a boy. Boyd spent the next few years wandering from job to job. He was dissatisfied, but didn't know how to turn his life around. During this time, Boyd's father retired from a long and successful career with the Toronto police department. The contrast between Boyd and his father was glaring; while Boyd senior settled into a comfortable retirement following 25 years of solid duty at the same job, his son continued to spin his wheels.

In April of 1949, Boyd turned 35. He was no longer a carefree young man who was able to bum across Canada if he wanted to. He had a family and he felt like a failure because he couldn't support them in style.

As the months passed, Boyd was feeling increasingly bitter and alienated. He began to consider returning to a life of crime. Perhaps now that he was a mature adult he wouldn't make amateur mistakes and get caught, as he had when he was younger. In the summer of 1949, Boyd read an article in a newspaper that helped him to make up his mind. The story concerned a teenage bank robber who had pulled off a huge heist. The teen, who was mentally handicapped, had strolled into a downtown Toronto bank and announced that he was robbing the place. He hadn't had a gun, but the intimidated bank clerks didn't hesitate to hand him stacks of cash. By the time the teenager left the bank, he was carrying nearly $70,000, an enormous sum at the time. The adolescent almost got away with the loot, but he had taken his time making an escape. Police had nabbed him as he casually made his way down the street, carrying the proceeds of his robbery.

Upon finishing the article, a flabbergasted Boyd put his newspaper down. He hadn't realized it was so easy to hold up a bank. With careful planning, he might be able to pull off a robbery of his own!

Boyd began to weigh the pros and cons of the bank robbing business. On the one hand, he had never committed anything more serious than car theft and breaking into a gas station; stealing money from a bank was an altogether larger and riskier proposition. Then again, Boyd already had all he needed for pulling off a heist: he had several years of military training, was extremely fit, and even possessed a nice pair of weapons. Best of all, bank robbing offered the opportunity to earn a great deal of money in a short period of time. At some point in the summer of 1949, Boyd made a momentous decision: he would start robbing banks to feed his family.

Having made up his mind, Boyd began looking

around for a suitable target. He settled on the Armour Heights branch of the Bank of Montreal. With the bank picked out, he started to plot his debut caper. He rented a garage, then visited the bank to familiarize himself with the layout and staff. Boyd also began to experiment with various ways of disguising himself. He discovered that wearing his wife's makeup and shoving cotton batting in his cheeks and nose dramatically altered his appearance. Wanting to look as little like himself as possible, Boyd also grew a moustache in anticipation of the heist. Everything was set. Now, to make the final leap from honest citizen to armed bank robber, he just needed one thing: courage.

* * *

On the morning of September 9, 1949, Edwin Boyd woke up, rolled out of bed, and got ready to rob his first bank. The former soldier began his preparations by disguising himself. He shoved wads of cotton into his cheeks and nostrils, smeared black mascara on his eyebrows, and rubbed rouge makeup on his cheeks. He then put on a hat and a dark-blue suit, and carefully positioned his pistol — the Luger he had picked up in France — under his suit jacket.

Once his physical transformation was complete,

Boyd spent the next portion of the morning gulping back shots of whiskey to fortify his nerves. He did this while sitting in the cab of his truck, which was parked in the garage he had rented near the bank. By the time Boyd was done drinking, half the bottle was gone and he was as drunk as he'd ever been. He wasn't nervous anymore, but he wasn't sober either. Staggering out of the garage, he made his way to the Bank of Montreal on foot. Even in his intoxicated state, Boyd knew better not to drive a vehicle to the bank. The truck might be seen by witnesses who could give a detailed description — and a license plate number — to police.

An unsteady Boyd walked through the door of the Armor Heights branch of the Bank of Montreal and stood in centre of the room, trying not to pass out. He felt drunk, so drunk that he was close to collapsing on the floor. As he fought to stay in control, he began to draw attention from staff.

Bank manager George Elwood eyed Boyd with suspicion. Elwood wondered if there was something wrong with the man. He looked odd and reeked of alcohol. Perhaps he was a hobo or a drunk who had wandered in off the street. Eager to get the strange man out of his bank, Elwood approached Boyd and asked if he could help him. By way of reply, Boyd handed Elwood a white sack and a folded cheque. Written on the cheque were the words HOLD UP, and below those words was an order to fill the sack with money. Boyd pulled his suit jacket open to display his pistol, and Elwood hurriedly told a female teller to fill the sack with cash.

Unnoticed by Boyd, the teller hit a silent alarm with her foot before starting to stuff cash into the bag. The alarm was connected to a nearby police station. Hoping to delay Boyd until the law arrived, she placed money in the sack as slowly as she could.

As she carried out her task, Boyd took the Luger from his belt and held it in his hands. He wasn't sure if he was prepared to use the gun, but he wasn't taking any chances.

After a few minutes had passed, Boyd decided he couldn't stay in the bank any longer. He grabbed the sack — which was filled with just over $2000 — and made a break for it. Waving his Luger at the bank staff, Boyd careened outside. The sun was blinding after the dim light inside the bank. Squinting in the brightness, he looked for a car to steal so he could escape before the police arrived. For all of his elaborate planning, Boyd hadn't put much thought into acquiring a getaway car. He had figured he would just hijack the first vehicle he came across, drive back to his garage, then get in his truck and go home.

Boyd spotted a blue sedan just a few metres away,

and headed towards it. A salesman named William Cranfield, who had been conducting some business at a store near the bank, owned the sedan. Cranfield was sitting in the driver's seat, getting ready to drive away, when Boyd's puffed up visage suddenly appeared in his passenger side window.

"Get out of the car!" Boyd ordered in a drunken voice as he grabbed Cranfield's car keys. Cranfield looked at the Luger in Boyd's hand and did as he was told. The salesman surrendered his vehicle and Boyd sat down in the driver's seat.

But as Boyd fiddled with the car keys, George Elwood came charging out of the bank waving a revolver. Back in the 1940s and 1950s, banks in Canada routinely stocked pistols to deter armed robbers. Bank employees were expected to train with the weapons, and even use them in the event of a robbery. In fact, it wasn't unusual for employees to shoot back at hold-up men.

The gun in Elwood's hand was a five-shot .38 caliber revolver. It was the kind of pistol detectives liked to use because it was small, reliable, and easy to conceal. It wasn't a powerful weapon, but at close range it did the trick. Standing only a few metres away from Boyd, Elwood levelled his revolver and squeezed the trigger. The muzzle flashed red as bullets began flying in Boyd's general direction. However, the man at the receiving end of Elwood's barrage was too drunk to notice he was being shot at. Boyd continued to awkwardly crank the key in the ignition switch, trying in his inebriated state to get the engine to start.

An irate Elwood began screaming that the bank had been robbed and that the robber was sitting in the sedan in front of him. Bullets from Elwood's .38 slammed into the car, tearing holes in its body. Cranfield dove for cover as Elwood unloaded his gun. But all of Elwood's shots missed their target, who remained absorbed in his efforts to start the car.

After a few more tries, Boyd gave up. He dashed out of the sedan and started running. As drunk as he was, he had no problem outrunning the furious bank manager. Boyd ran through people's backyards, over fences, and down alleys. A few people cursed at him for trespassing on their property, but Boyd simply muttered excuses at them and hurried on his way.

Amazingly, Boyd was successful in evading capture. At some point, he stopped running and began walking calmly down the street. When no one was looking, Boyd took out the cotton batting he had stuffed in his mouth and nose and tossed it away. He rubbed some of the makeup off his face and affected a casual gait, like a man out for a stroll. As he walked, police cars whizzed by, sirens blaring, on their way the Bank of Montreal. If any of the drivers noticed Boyd, they didn't bother to stop and interrogate him. After all, they were looking for a puffy-faced hold-up man. Now that he had gotten rid of his disguise and stopped running, Boyd looked like any bystander. No one would have thought he was a bank robber carrying the proceeds from his first successful heist.

Boyd carefully made his way back to his rented garage. Climbing into his truck, he decided to take a quick nap. All the liquor and running had worn him out. He slept for a few minutes then woke up and counted his loot. It came to $2256. Back in 1949, a single Canadian dollar was worth roughly eight times what it is today. Boyd's haul was worth about $18,000 by today's standards — not a huge amount, but impressive enough for one day's work.

Despite several near-disasters, Boyd had gotten away with his first bank heist. He smiled as he counted the money again. Bank robbing was looking like a much more profitable line of work than driving a streetcar. It was also looking like a more illustrious one.

Boyd became an instant media celebrity. The day after he robbed the Bank of Montreal, Toronto papers were filled with lurid accounts of his exploits. At that time, the three biggest newspapers in town were the

A Career Switch

Globe and Mail, the *Toronto Daily Star,* and the now defunct *Toronto Telegram.* The *Star* and the *Telegram* had long been locked in a bitter competition to attract readers. Both papers featured Boyd's debut robbery on their front pages, although the *Telegram*'s headline, "Bank Bandit Escapes 6 Shots, Gets $2000," got the facts slightly mixed up.

In order to attract more readers, and therefore more advertising, the *Star* and the *Telegram* vied to outdo each other with news "scoops" about sin, corruption, and larceny in Toronto. One of the most legendary newsroom figures at the time was a man named Gwyn "Jocko" Thomas. A hard-hitting, hard-driving reporter, Jocko Thomas worked for the *Toronto Star.* He had a punchy style, and knew how to turn an ordinary stickup into a major media event. Jocko could conduct interviews on the fly and file stories fast — a good thing, too, as papers typically ran several editions during a single day, depending on how exciting the news was.

Jocko cavorted with cops and criminals alike. Wherever there was a crime scene, especially a serious crime scene, the local constabulary could be sure that Jocko Thomas would show up to investigate. Of course, in those days, there were not a lot of serious crimes to report; armed robberies were rare in Toronto during the 1940s and 1950s. A robbery in broad daylight by a single gunman might not have attracted much attention in Chicago or New York, but in Toronto, it was a sensation.

Boyd was pleasantly surprised by all the media attention. While he had expected to make a lot of money on his first robbery, he hadn't anticipated becoming famous in the process. Still, Boyd wasn't vain enough to think he was a brilliant bank robber. He had gotten away with his first heist out of sheer luck.

In the days following the Bank of Montreal job, Boyd carefully analyzed all the mistakes he had made during the robbery. Getting drunk had been idiotic. The whisky had nearly knocked Boyd out. He had been so far gone that he hadn't known Elwood was shooting at him until he'd read about it in the papers. The booze had also made him sleepy and unfocussed, two conditions that are best avoided while trying to pull off a heist. Boyd decided that he would never again mix booze with bank robbery. He also decided that the next time he robbed a bank, he'd have a getaway car on hand so that he could make a speedy escape.

Boyd waited several weeks before pulling another hold up. Once again, he rented a garage. He also stole a car well in advance of the robbery. For his getaway vehicle, Boyd choose a blue 1949 Meteor. The criminal skills he had picked up during his youth continued to prove their worth. Stealing cars was child's play for Boyd.

A Career Switch

On January 18, 1950, Boyd drove the Meteor to a Canadian Bank of Commerce located at O'Connor Drive and St. Clair Avenue East. He was dressed in old, torn clothes, and had once again stuffed his cheeks full of cotton batting. Boyd had been watching the bank carefully long before robbery day. He knew that the manager left the building shortly after noon each day to eat his lunch in an apartment right above the bank. Boyd waited until the manager went upstairs, then entered the bank.

Just as he had done at the Bank of Montreal, Boyd passed an employee a folded cheque to that bore the words, HOLD UP written in pencil. Boyd waited to see the employee's reaction then removed his Luger pistol from his belt. Once he had gotten everyone's attention, he handed the employee a sugar sack and demanded that it be filled with cash.

Boyd remembered how the teller at the Bank of Montreal had deliberately dawdled, filling up his sack as slowly as possible. He had been too drunk at the time to realize that she had been stalling, hoping to cause a long delay so police could nab him. Now that he was sober and in full command of his senses, Boyd ordered the teller to move quickly. She obeyed, and the sugar sack was rapidly filled with bills.

Once the sack was sufficiently heavy, Boyd ordered the bank employees into the vault then raced outside and jumped into his getaway car. He gunned the Meteor's engine and tore down the street. Boyd was in and out of the Canadian Bank of Commerce in minutes. And this time, there had been no trouble with the bank manager and no problems starting the getaway car. Everything had gone much more smoothly than it had during his first robbery.

After driving for a few kilometres, Boyd got rid of the Meteor and continued on foot. He knew that the police would be on the lookout for the car and he didn't want to risk being pulled over and captured. Sure enough, police quickly located the Meteor, which Boyd had abandoned near a disposal plant in East York. In fact, a patrol car came across the vehicle within minutes of Boyd ditching it. Once again, luck was on Boyd's side.

Boyd was blessed by a second stroke of good fortune. The day he committed his second robbery, it was snowing heavily in Toronto. Visibility was poor and driving conditions were hazardous. The snow slowed the police down and made it easier for Boyd to slip through the city unnoticed.

Cautiously, Boyd made his way back to his home and family, and counted his money. His take on the Canadian Bank of Commerce job was $2862, worth about $22,000 by today's standards. While this second haul wasn't huge, Boyd's exploits took up many more column inches this time around. In their descriptions to police, some of the Bank of Commerce employees claimed Boyd was "hopped up" on drugs. As a result, the *Toronto Star* referred to Boyd as a "dope crazed bank bandit" and splashed his heist on the front page.

By this time, Dorreen had discovered her husband's new vocation. Boyd had expected her to be furious, but instead, her reaction was strangely cool. She seemed to accept the fact her husband was now a criminal. Maybe she was unscrupulous, or maybe she was just a pragmatist. Either way, she was a war bride in an unfamiliar country, with three children to look after. Going to the police would have left Dorreen stranded and on her own, thousands of kilometres from England, with a family to support.

Relieved by his wife's acceptance of his abrupt career switch, Boyd began plotting new capers. It was an exciting time for him; he had finally found a job he was good at. Even better, it was a job that paid well. For someone who worried about his station in life as much as Edwin Boyd, bank robbing was proving to be a rewarding occupation.

* * *

Boyd's first two bank robberies set the pattern for his

future stick-ups. For both early heists, Boyd had rented a garage near the scene of his crime. He had also chosen banks located in suburban locales instead of ones situated closer to downtown. The reasons for this were twofold. First of all, there weren't as many cops in suburbia, and their stations were spread farther apart. Secondly, making a quick escape in a getaway car was easier on suburban streets because traffic was always less congested. For these reasons, Boyd continued to target suburban banks.

In the summer of 1950, Boyd tried a new approach to his work when he used a partner for the first time. The identity of this partner remains a mystery. All that is known about the man is that he helped Boyd rob the Dominion Bank on Glencairn Avenue and Dufferin Street in early July of 1950.

On the day of this particular heist, Boyd, who had deliberately neglected to shave, slapped makeup on his face and put on a blue suit and straw hat. Then, with the mystery accomplice in tow, he sauntered into the Dominion Bank and proceeded to rob the place. To make his presence known, Boyd gave a shout and leapt on top of the bank counter. Flushed with adrenaline, he waved his gun at the frightened staff. No one dared resist his demands, and Boyd and his partner bagged $1954, as well as a bank issue .38 caliber revolver. Prior to the stick-up, Boyd had stolen a Ford convertible to use as a getaway vehicle. Following the robbery, Boyd and his partner drove the stolen convertible a safe distance away from the bank, and then ditched it in a swamp near Lawrence Avenue. Police located the convertible but found no trace of the two bank robbers.

Though the Dominion Bank robbery had been successful, Boyd had mixed feelings about the heist and its outcome. On the one hand, it had been surprisingly easy. Having a partner to back him up had taken a lot of pressure off him. But then again, the pair had made off with less than $2000, and that had to be split two ways. Boyd wasn't happy that he had to share such a paltry sum. Feeling frustrated, he decided flying solo was preferable. He would go back to holding up banks by himself, at least for the time being.

In the fall of 1950, Boyd selected the Imperial Bank in North York as his next target. At the time, North York consisted of scattered residential neighbourhoods and farmland, ideal territory for making a fast getaway in a car. As usual, Boyd had stolen a vehicle in preparation for the heist. On the day of the robbery, he parked it outside the bank and went to work.

The Imperial Bank was nearly deserted when Boyd stepped inside. He took a quick glance around, pulled out his Luger, and announced that a hold up was in progress. But as it turned out, the bank manager, a man by the name W.H.G. Smith, was not about to tolerate such an announcement. Instead of meekly complying with Boyd's demands, Smith snatched a bank-issue revolver from his desk and started shooting. Soon, the bank was filled with the smell of hot gunpowder as Smith and Boyd exchanged rounds at almost point-blank range. Incredibly, not a single shot found its mark. His Luger still smoking from the impromptu gun battle, Boyd raced out of the Imperial Bank and back to his stolen vehicle. He drove off, having made no money at all.

Later that autumn, Boyd found legitimate employment as a street repair worker with the City of Toronto. His job was to scoop asphalt into potholes. Though the position didn't pay well and the work was hot and sticky, Boyd was content with his job because it gave him plenty of time to think. During the brief period he spent on the road crew, Boyd hatched an audacious scheme. He would return to the scene of his first bank heist — the Armor Heights branch of the Bank of Montreal — and rob the place again. Ever the show-off, Boyd found the notion of robbing the same place twice very appealing.

On March 19, 1951, Boyd put his plan into action. Working alone again, he stole a black Chevrolet, stuffed his cheeks with cotton batting, and drove to the bank. Lucky for Boyd, George Elwood was not working on the day of the second heist. Elwood was ill, and thus missed his chance to chase Boyd down the street again.

Upon entering the bank, Boyd pulled out his gun and demanded cash. This time, there was no bank manager willing to get in his way. Staff cooperated with all of Boyd's demands. He cleaned out the cash drawers then flamboyantly leapt over the bank counter to make his getaway. One of the tellers at the Bank of Montreal recognized Boyd as the man who had robbed them two years earlier. This fact was cited in all the newspaper coverage of the heist. The *Telegram* ran a huge front-page headline reading, "Robs Bank 2nd Time, Adds $5000 to Loot". Once more, the papers got their figures wrong; Boyd had made off with about $3000.

To keep busy and make some money on the side, Boyd continued to work as a street repairman. In the course of his labours, he became friendly with a fellow employee named Howard Gault. Gault was 42 years old, out of shape, a heavy drinker, and not terribly bright. Still, Boyd figured he might make an ideal partner. Indeed, Gault was very similar to Boyd in several ways. Like Boyd, Gault had spent much of his life drifting aimlessly from casual job to casual job. He, too, was a family man, albeit not a very devoted one; prior to meeting Boyd, Gault had deserted his wife and two kids. While Boyd had served in the army, Gault had once worked as a prison guard, so he was familiar with guns. Most importantly, Gault was already a petty criminal. He revealed to Boyd that he liked to steal from parked cars to earn extra drinking money. Boyd smiled when he heard this news, then suggested the pair go after bigger game. Gault went along with Boyd's suggestion. Earning money through crime seemed preferable to heaping tar on city roads.

After securing Gault's services, Boyd went about recruiting another partner. This time he set his sights on his younger brother, Norman Boyd. Like Gault, Norman had never robbed a bank, nor had he really considered trying to. But big brother Boyd was very persuasive. He cited his string of successful hold ups and made robbery sound easy. Once again, Boyd's charm and fast-talk had its intended effect, and Norman agreed to participate in the hold up.

On September 1, 1951, the two Boyd brothers and Gault set out to rob the Dominion Bank on Sheppard Avenue East. The threesome stole a 1950 Mercury and drove it to their intended target. As per usual, the bank was located on the fringes of Toronto. Feeling confident in their plan, the three men entered the bank and conducted a methodical robbery. As befitting a former military man, Boyd had given everyone clearly defined tasks; Boyd forced the bank staff into the vault at gunpoint, Gault scooped up as much money as he could grab from the cash drawers, and Norman guarded the door.

Working systematically, the team made off with $8029 in a matter of minutes. It was Boyd's biggest score yet.

The Dominion Bank robbery proved to be a turning point for Boyd. For the first time in his life, he had commanded his own team of armed robbers. It was a heady moment for the former rail-riding hobo. In spite of all the excitement, Boyd was wise enough to keep a low profile after the Dominion hold up. He wasn't the type to flash money around or go on spending sprees that might attract attention. Instead, he used the proceeds of his crimes to treat his family to movies, meals, or special shows like the circus. Only allowing himself these small pleasures, Boyd led an unostentatious lifestyle.

Following the Dominion Bank robbery, Boyd decided to drop even further from public scrutiny. He packed up his family and moved them to Pickering, Ontario, which, at the time, was a more or less rural area just outside of Toronto. The house Boyd bought in Pickering was particularly rustic. To Dorreen and the children's dismay, it didn't even have running water. Situated on a big, empty meadow that could have been mistaken for a farmer's field, the new Boyd residence was a loveless cinderblock building that looked like something the army would use to store ammunition in.

But while Dorreen and the children might have been lacking for companions and creature comforts in their new home, the location of the house suited Boyd's needs perfectly. It was close to Toronto, which would allow him to get in and out of the city quickly. At the same time, it was isolated, which meant he didn't have to worry about the prying eyes of his neighbours.

But for all his caution, Boyd still had a taste for the sensational. In October of 1951, he made a reckless decision: he would rob the Bank of Montreal at Armour Heights a third time. Throughout his criminal career, Boyd had vacillated between conducting carefully planned robberies and spur-of-the-moment heists. He approached his third attempt on the Armour Heights Bank of Montreal with an almost casual air.

Having been robbed twice in two years, staff at the bank would surely be on the lookout for possible criminals. Nonetheless, Boyd undertook his latest bank job with very little preparation. He put on his disguise, stole a 1948 black Chevrolet, and, with Gault in tow, drove the vehicle to the Armour Heights district.

As soon as the stolen Chevy began cruising in front of the bank, employees became suspicious. They called the police and told them about the dodgy looking vehicle idling by their front window. Upon glancing inside the bank, Boyd noticed the attention he was drawing from the employees and drove away at a fast clip. In later interviews, Boyd openly regretted that he hadn't just gone home that day and forgotten about robbing banks for a while. But Gault had been travelling with him, and was severely disappointed by their failure to follow through with a heist. He began arguing with Boyd, demanding that they try somewhere else. After all, they had guns and a getaway car; all they needed was a new target.

Despite his misgivings, Boyd gave in to Gault's pleading. The two men drove to a Dominion Bank on Yonge Street and Lawrence Avenue. They parked the car and entered the bank with their guns drawn, like members of an outlaw gang from the Old West.

"This is a stick-up!" Boyd shouted as he jumped on the counter. Holding the bank employees at gunpoint, he waited for Gault to take the money from the tellers' cages and place it in a shopping bag. But instead of carrying out his usual job, Gault started to throw the money in the air. Boyd and the bank employees watched in confused amazement as Gault grabbed fistfuls of bills and tossed them about like confetti.

Suddenly it dawned on Boyd that Gault was drunk.

Boyd had been able to pull off a bank job while inebriated, albeit barely. Gault, however, was out of control. He wasn't listening to Boyd, who kept telling him to smarten up and stop playing with the cash. In all the chaos, neither man noticed that an employee had activated a silent alarm. Police began converging on the bank as Boyd hissed at his partner to get a move on.

Finally, Boyd managed to convince Gault to leave. The pair raced outside, making it to the sidewalk just as a police cruiser and an officer on a motorcycle were pulling up to the bank. His heart pounding, Boyd sprinted to the stolen Chevy with a cop hot on his tail. He opened the car door and slammed it into the officer, knocking the wind out of him. With the officer doubled over, Boyd leapt inside the car, started the engine, and raced off. Regaining his composure, the winded constable drew his revolver and fired wildly into the street after the Chevrolet. Boyd gunned the engine and escaped into traffic.

That would have been the end of the whole unnerving experience for Boyd if not for one thing: Gault hadn't made it to the Chevrolet. Brandishing his .38, Gault had tried to flee on foot. But unlike Boyd, Gault was no athlete. He managed to put just a short distance between himself and the bank when the policeman on the motorcycle drew his weapon and fired a pair of warning shots into the air. Gault stopped running as soon as he heard the gunshots. Out of breath, he let his .38 fall to the ground, along with a shopping bag that contained over $12,000 of stolen cash from the Dominion Bank. Police grabbed the gun and the money and placed Gault under arrest.

Gault was taken to a nearby police station, where he proved to be a most helpful informant. Not one to follow the credo "honour among thieves," he told the cops everything he knew about Boyd and the string of robberies he had committed. Boyd, meanwhile, was doing his best to evade the police and get back home to Pickering. He had ditched the stolen Chevy and was continuing on in his own truck. But as he sped towards his family, a pair of detectives from the auto squad intercepted him. The detectives had been given a description of Boyd's truck — courtesy of Gault — and were patrolling along York Mills Road when they caught sight of the vehicle they were looking for.

The detective at the wheel of the pursuit car drove up alongside Boyd's truck. Once the car was in line with the truck, the officer on the passenger side rolled down his window and aimed his gun at Boyd's face. Both detectives barked warnings at Boyd, yelling at him not to do anything stupid. Boyd still had his Luger tucked into his belt, but he didn't reach for it. With a gun pointed at his head, such a move would have been suicidal. Instead, he played it cool and let himself be captured. He didn't protest when the detectives searched his truck, and he even managed to sound casual when he inquired about Gault. Of course, an answer from the officers wasn't forthcoming.

Boyd was taken to Toronto police headquarters, where officers subjected him to a round of intense interrogations. Years later, Boyd would claim that the police slapped him around and threatened even more physical violence if he didn't confess. Whatever the case, Boyd soon admitted to pulling a number of armed robberies, and on October 17, 1951, he was sent to Toronto's notorious Don Jail. Facing a long stretch behind bars for his various misdeeds, Boyd's criminal life seemed to be over.

Chapter 4
Don Jail Blues

F or all of Edwin Boyd's bravado, the thought of being held in the Don Jail made him deeply uneasy. As every criminal knew, the Don was the worst possible place in Toronto to be locked up in. The jail was opened in 1864 and still exists today. Situated on a hilltop in the eastern part of the city, it overlooks the expansive Don Valley and is oppressively gloomy. The outside walls of the Don Jail are a pallid shade of yellow. The cells inside the prison are tiny and were made that way deliberately; the idea was that a small, enclosed space would give prisoners plenty of opportunity to contemplate their misdeeds. Almost always filled to capacity and beyond, the Don Jail was denounced as "an overcrowded dungeon" by a Toronto grand jury in 1935. The *Toronto Star* later referred to the Don as the city's "Medieval Prison".

At the time Boyd entered the Don, the prisoner population stood at about 450 inmates, far more than the facility could hold comfortably. Many of the men there had only been charged but not convicted of various crimes. This meant the wrongly accused had to rub shoulders with hardened cons.

Boyd was placed on the second floor of the Don Jail in a cell that was just over six feet long by six feet wide. The cell was located off a long a corridor with 18 other cells. As he lay in his tiny space listening to the echo of footsteps on the prison's stone floor, Boyd's spirits continued to fall. Wanting more than anything to get out of jail, he claimed to be remorseful and insisted that he wanted to clean up his act.

Perhaps if he had been placed near inmates who were equally contrite, Boyd would have "gone straight" after serving his sentence. As it was, the presence of two prisoners in nearby cells practically guaranteed that Boyd would return to a life of crime. The prisoners were Lennie Jackson and Willie Jackson, two men with a history of committing violent offences. Though they had the same last name, the men were not related.

Lennie Jackson was taller than Boyd, and had black hair and dark, brooding features. Always polite and well spoken, Lennie harboured a hot temper and a violent nature that earned him the nickname "Tough Lennie." Like Boyd, Lennie had served in the Canadian Forces during World War II. His health had always been precarious, however, and he was discharged from the army in June of 1944. Among other medical problems, Lennie suffered terribly from asthma.

Two years after his discharge, Lennie had a serious accident that left him partly disabled. While trying to hop onto a freight car near downtown Toronto, he slipped and fell under the moving train. His left foot was severed as a result. Lennie spent months in hospital recuperating from the accident, and had to wear an artificial foot after his release.

Upon getting out of hospital, Lennie worked occasionally as a waiter at the Horseshoe Tavern. The Horseshoe was a favourite haunt for Toronto criminals and lowlifes. Police routinely dropped by the place to keep tabs on the activities of local miscreants. Lenny, of course, was one of those miscreants. Even though he had a legitimate job, he had few scruples about committing serious crimes on the side. In fact, just like Boyd, he too had been arrested for robbing banks.

Willie Jackson was far less intense than Lennie.

Edwin Alonzo Boyd

Standing five foot seven with soft features and a receding hairline, Willie loved to drink alcohol and make people laugh. A natural born clown, Willie's genial appearance masked a vicious nature. In the summer of 1948, he was sent to the Kingston Penitentiary for mugging two men at different Toronto locations. Upon his release in 1951, he beat an old man senseless with a beer bottle and was given seven years for this crime. But while Willie's violent actions were upsetting to most ordinary citizens, his criminal companions didn't seem to care; they were more interested in his jokes than his shady past. Even the Don guards thought Willie was good for a laugh.

As Boyd became friendly with the Jacksons, the three men began to talk about the possibilities of breaking out of jail. Lennie revealed that he had smuggled a hacksaw blade into the Don in his artificial foot. Somehow the guards had overlooked the foot during their searches. Lennie wanted to use his blade to cut through the bars on a window in the corridor. The window looked out onto the Don's exercise yard and was protected by a wire screen. Behind the screen was a frosted pane of glass that could be opened to let in air, and behind the glass were the bars Lennie wanted to cut.

Lennie asked Boyd to help with the escape plan, and Boyd happily consented. It was decided that Boyd and Willie would work on sawing the window bars while Lennie — along with any other prisoners in the corridor who knew about the escape plan — would keep an eye out for guards. To get at the bars, Boyd and Willie removed a bolt from the wire screen that was protecting the window, and then pushed the screen upwards. The men then slipped under the screen, climbed over the glass pane, and sawed at the bars. Because the Don Jail was so old, the steel bars were relatively soft and malleable. With enough time, it would be possible to saw through the steel even with the small hacksaw blade. Every day, Boyd and Willie would take turns sawing at the bars. They concealed the nicks and cuts in the bars by rubbing them with soap and dirt.

By early November of 1951, the bars were nearly cut through. It was time for Boyd, Lennie, and Willie to put the rest of their escape plan into motion. To prepare for their breakout, the three men fashioned two ropes out of sheets taken from several cells. One rope was roughly 50 feet long, the other much shorter. Once the ropes were ready, Boyd was sent under the wire screen and over the frosted glass pane. He sawed through the remainder of the bar he had been working on, then glanced down at the exercise yard 40 feet below. The ground was covered in a dusting of snow, but to Boyd, it still looked warm and inviting.

Boyd tied one end of the long rope around one of the remaining bars and tossed the rest of the rope out into the exercise yard. Then, like a mountaineer rappelling down a cliff, he used the rope to climb down from the window. Lennie and Willie followed without trouble, and all three men made their way across the exercise yard, their feet crunching in the snow. They moved cautiously to one of the jail's outer walls, a stone structure that stood over 16 feet high. Boyd and Lennie positioned themselves next to the wall, and Willie climbed on top of them, putting his feet on their shoulders. He swung the shorter rope like a lasso and secured one end to a cornice on top of the wall. Willie then pulled himself up, followed by Boyd and Lennie. There was a 10-foot drop from the top of the wall to the snow-covered ground on the other side. With no time to hesitate, the men jumped off the wall and landed safely. Even Lennie, with his artificial foot, made it to the ground without difficulty.

Though they had escaped the prison grounds successfully, the three men knew they were not home free just yet. They needed to get as far away from the Don Jail as possible. The men hurredly made their way to the snow-filled Don Valley, where one of Lennie's buddies was supposed to pick them up. This buddy, whose real name was Val Lesso, called himself Steve Suchan. Stocky and good-looking, Suchan had been a talented violinist as a child. He later gave up his musical ambitions for less savoury endeavours. In the spring of 1950, at the age of 22, Suchan was sent to the Guelph Reformatory for trying to pass forged checks. After his release, he traded his violin for a .455 revolver and turned to violent crime to make a living. Suchan started robbing banks with Lennie in March of 1951, and the two men pulled off several small town heists before Lennie was caught.

Now the plan was for Suchan to meet Lennie, Boyd, and Willie at a prearranged spot then drive them away in his car. But when the runaway trio made it to the established meeting point, Suchan was nowhere to be seen. After shivering in the Don Valley for some time, Lennie scouted out a phone and called the tardy pickup man. Suchan was staying at the home of his girlfriend, Anna Camero. When he took the call from Lennie he sounded apologetic and claimed he had forgotten when the escape was scheduled. Suchan then drove out to the valley, picked the men up, and deposited them at Camero's house on Toronto's Wright Avenue.

They had done it. Lennie Jackson, Willie Jackson, and Edwin Boyd had escaped from the notorious Don Jail.

Chapter 5
The Boyd Gang

Immediately following their escape from the Don Jail, Boyd and the two Jacksons did their best to keep a low profile. Lennie reunited with his girlfriend, Ann Roberts, and took up residence at a tourist camp near Oshawa. Willie and Boyd, meanwhile, stayed at a boarding house owned by Steve Suchan's parents, Joseph and Elizabeth Lesso. Joseph and Elizabeth had emigrated to Canada from Czechoslovakia and neither spoke much English.

After settling in at the Lessos', Boyd took stock of his situation. Figuring the police had his Pickering house under surveillance, he did not dare contact his

The Boyd Gang

family. Instead, he plotted a fresh caper. Just a few short days after escaping from the Don Jail, Boyd, along with the two Jacksons and Suchan, robbed the Bank of Toronto at Dundas and Boustead. They took $4300, and once again, Boyd's name was plastered across local newspapers. "The gang is believed by police to have been led by Edwin Alonzo Boyd, master bank robber, who escaped with two other desperate criminals from the Don Jail two weeks ago," wrote Jocko Thomas in the *Toronto Star.*

In his article, Jocko referred to the group of bank robbers as "The Boyd Gang." It was a catchy title, and it stuck. Lennie wasn't impressed. He considered himself the real leader of the gang. But no matter who led and who followed, all four men agreed to continue working together. Just one week after the Bank of Toronto heist, the Boyd Gang was poised to strike again. In preparation for their next job, Boyd stole a blue Ford sedan. He and the others then used this vehicle to conduct what was, at the time, the largest successful bank heist in the history of Toronto.

The gang selected the Royal Bank of Canada on Laird Drive as their target. As usual, Boyd leapt on the counter to announce the start of the robbery. While Boyd waved a revolver in the air, Suchan entered the bank through the back entrance and captured the bank manager in his office. He took out a pistol and herded the startled manager to the front of the building to join a line-up of stunned employees. As Suchan kept an eye on the employees, Willie and Boyd began to transfer the contents of the cash drawers into a pair of pillowcases. Lennie, meanwhile, stood guard at the front door with a submachine gun. Wearing an overcoat and fedora, Lennie looked just like a Hollywood gangster. For their efforts, the four men made off with $46,270, the equivalent of about $360,000 today.

Their back-to-back robberies turned the Boyd Gang into criminal superstars. Edwin Boyd's exploits were no longer just grist for the local press; the gang bearing his name was now known throughout the country. Newspaper accounts of the Boyd Gang made them sound like an extremely well organized criminal outfit. But in reality, the gang members didn't get along particularly well. Boyd and Suchan disliked each other immensely. Like Lennie, Suchan was envious of Boyd's position within the group. He felt that Boyd was an interloper who was trying to get between him and Lennie. Willie, on the other hand, got along with everyone. He was light-hearted and seemed to enjoy being a bank robber. During his stay at the Suchan boarding house, Willie got closer to Boyd, and even grew to respect his leadership style.

The Boyd Gang

For all their internal difficulties, the members of the Boyd Gang couldn't help but be impressed by the headlines they were inspiring. Among the most notable was a front-page banner in the *Toronto Star* that read "Sten Gun Five Stage Biggest Bank Hold-up in History of Toronto." The Sten Gun belonged to Lennie. The "five" were really four, but then, such mistakes were typical in coverage of Boyd's crimes.

The huge amount of media coverage the Gang generated has to be considered within the context of the times. During the early 1950s, Toronto had a reputation for being upright and uptight; it was known as a city of churches, not criminal gangs. The sheer audacity of robbing banks in such a locale sparked a huge amount of interest in the Boyd Gang's activities.

For all their newfound fame, the Boyd Gang proved to be just as capable of being fleeced as any bank manager. While staying at the Lessos' boarding house, Boyd and Willie needed to find a place to hide their bank loot. By this point, Suchan's father had figured out that his son's new friends were not ordinary working men. Insisting that he wanted to help his guests out, Joseph Lesso persuaded Boyd to hide his bank loot under some floorboards inside the boarding house. Boyd figured this hiding spot was as good as any, so he handed his money over to the old man and convinced Willie to do the same.

The next morning, Boyd and Willie found the boarding house in turmoil. Suchan's father was gone, and Suchan was yelling at his mother in Slovak. Mrs. Lesso apparently had no idea where her husband was, and Suchan didn't know either. Joseph Lesso had disappeared, along with most of Boyd and Willie's money. Infuriated, Willie threatened Suchan's mother with a .45 pistol, an action that terrified the woman, angered Suchan, and did nothing to bring the men closer to getting their money back. But while Willie was livid, Boyd took the loss with stoic resignation. As far as he was concerned, money was never a problem; if he ran out, he would just rob another bank.

In December of 1951, Suchan and Lennie travelled to Montreal with Lennie's sister, Mary Mitchell. Lennie was dropped off at a rooming house where girlfriend Ann Roberts was waiting for him. Suchan and Mary Mitchell, meanwhile, signed a lease on an apartment that was located in a respectable, middle-class neighbourhood. Even though Suchan already had a girlfriend, he was becoming romantically involved with Mary. The two of them registered for their apartment as husband and wife. During this time, Suchan also purchased a new Chrysler.

Later that month, Boyd and Willie travelled to Montreal as well. Staying at a hotel under false names, they weren't in the city long before Willie let his rambunctious nature get the better of him. Just days before Christmas, Willie went to a Montreal nightclub where he proceeded to get drunk. The more he drank, the louder and rowdier he became. Soon, he was flashing a .45 revolver to impress his fellow patrons, and not surprisingly, someone called the authorities.

Police arrived at the Montreal nightclub and arrested Willie. In addition to a fully loaded revolver, he had 20 rounds of ammunition on him. It didn't take long for authorities to figure out he was one of the three men who had escaped from the Don Jail a few weeks earlier. Suspecting that Willie was part of the Boyd Gang, police were anxious to find out where the organization's ringleader was hiding. But unlike Boyd's former partner, Gault, Willie didn't squeal. He denied knowing the whereabouts of Boyd, Lennie, or Suchan.

In late 1951, Willie was sentenced to two years in jail for escaping from the Don. This was added to the seven-year sentence he was already serving for committing robbery with violence. Willie was shipped off to serve his time in Kingston Penitentiary, leaving the rest of the gang without a fourth member.

Soon after Willie's arrest, Boyd returned to Toronto and got a room at the Sunnyside Motor Hotel. There, he and his family were reunited, and they celebrated

Christmas together. Boyd played with his three children and opened presents with Dorreen. It was a rare, happy moment for a family whose chief breadwinner was on the run from the law.

Shortly after the New Year, Boyd found himself running low on funds. His solution, of course, was to find a new bank to rob. He picked the Bank of Toronto on Kingston Road and then went about contacting his remaining partners. Unfortunately for Boyd, the gang that bore his name was drifting into disarray.

Lennie and Suchan were still in Montreal and refused to come to Toronto to join Boyd in his latest robbery. Boyd was less than happy with this arrangement, but quickly located a fledgling thief who was willing to join the gang. The aspiring bank robber just happened to be Joseph Jackson, Willie's brother. Joseph lived in Toronto and was perfectly comfortable with the idea of committing armed robbery.

In the end, Suchan decided to travel to Toronto after all. He arrived in town with Mary Mitchell, who insisted on taking part in the robbery. The Boyd Gang had never included female partners before, but the men agreed to let her serve as one of their getaway drivers. On January 24, 1952, Boyd stole a black Ford sedan in anticipation of the robbery. One day later, Boyd, Suchan, and Joseph entered the Bank of Toronto, guns in hand. As usual, Boyd demanded full cooperation and all the money in the bank. And as usual, he was given both.

A few weeks after the Bank of Toronto heist, Boyd decided it was time to commit another robbery. He contacted his confederates, who had scattered once again. Suchan was back in Montreal with Lennie Jackson. Both men agreed to take part in Boyd's new caper, but on the day they were supposed to meet their erstwhile leader, neither of them showed up. Frustrated, Boyd decided to proceed without the two men. He approached Willie's brother Joseph, who was happy to help out for a second time. Joseph, in turn, convinced his brother-in-law, a man named Allister Gibson, to take part in the heist as well.

By this time, Boyd was thinking about retiring. His plan was to save enough money to purchase a rooming house. He would serve as landlord and primary owner of the house, but figured that if any of the Boyd Gang wanted to chip in, they could become part owners of the place.

In late February of 1952, Boyd set about stealing some cars for his next heist. Then, on a day in early March, Boyd, Joseph, and Allister Gibson drove to the Bank of Montreal on College and Manning streets. They burst inside and took out their guns. No one in the bank tried to play hero, and the three robbers netted $24,696 within a few short minutes. Boyd was pleased. A couple more easy scores like that and he'd be able to buy his rooming house and retire from the criminal life for good.

Chapter 6
Ambush

On January 1, 1952, Canada entered a new year and Toronto welcomed a new mayor. His name was Allan Lamport and he was a large, flamboyant man who fancied himself a crime-buster. Naturally, the Boyd Gang became an immediate target for the self-promoting politician.

If Lamport had a counterpart on the Toronto police force, it was Sergeant of Detectives Eddie Tong. Born in England, Detective Tong was a big, gregarious man who loved police work. He had a huge circle of informants and frequently visited local bars, including the Horseshoe Tavern, to pick up information.

Tong was very familiar with the Boyd Gang. In fact, he was using Mary Mitchell as an informant. Though no one can be sure why Mary was feeding the detective information, there is some suggestion that she did it as an act of spite against Suchan, who was still involved with Anna Camero. In February of 1952, Mary gave Tong the description and license plate number of Camero's car. The car was a 1951 black Monarch sedan with whitewall tires. Mary claimed that criminals were using the vehicle to transport stolen goods from Toronto to Montreal. Ever efficient, Detective Tong memorized the piece of information and filed it away.

At around 1 P.M. on March 6, 1952, Lennie Jackson and Steve Suchan borrowed Camero's black Monarch sedan to take a drive around Toronto. Both men were armed, but it's unclear if they were planning to rob a bank or whether they were just being cautious. The Boyd Gang, after all, were among the most wanted criminals in the country. But cautious or not, neither Lennie nor Suchan had any idea that Detective Tong was on the lookout for the very black Monarch they were driving. Tong was working that day, riding around the city in an unmarked cruiser with an officer by the name of Roy Perry. While patrolling Toronto's west end, Tong spotted Camero's black Monarch, and the two officers began to follow the vehicle.

Ambush

It's doubtful that Tong knew who was inside the car. Thanks to Mary Mitchell, however, he was aware that the vehicle was being used for criminal purposes. Tong told his partner he wanted to check the car out. The Monarch approached the intersection of College Street and Landsdowne Avenue, and began to slow down for a red light. As the vehicle came to a stop, Perry eased the police cruiser up next to the Monarch, and Tong rolled down his window and ordered the two men to pull over. The men obliged, and Tong stepped out of his cruiser and headed towards the black Monarch. Not suspecting trouble, Tong hadn't bothered to draw his gun. Detective Perry, for his part, wasn't even armed. He had left his weapon behind at the police station.

Inside the Monarch, Suchan and Lennie were tense with fear. Boyd was on the RCMP's Most Wanted list, and the members of his gang were considered only slightly less dangerous than he was. Suchan clutched the grip of his .455 Smith & Wesson revolver, ready for action.

Detective Tong was just a few feet away from the Monarch when a shot rang out. Suddenly, a bullet struck Tong in the chest and pierced his flesh. The round cut deep into the detective's body, severing his spinal cord. In an instant, Tong collapsed face-first on the road, perilously wounded. The large man hadn't even had a chance to draw his weapon.

Detective Perry gasped as his partner fell to the ground. Before he could radio for help, slugs began slamming through the windshield of the police car, spraying the officer with shards of glass. Perry raised his right arm to protect himself as he was peppered with glass and bullets. One round slammed into the detective's right arm, between his wrist and elbow. The officer screamed in pain as his arm went limp.

The barrage of shots ended, and Lennie, gun in hand, stepped out of the Monarch to survey the scene. When he saw Tong lying on the asphalt in front of him, Lennie leapt back into the car and ordered Suchan to drive. Suchan gunned the motor, leaving the two badly injured policemen at the intersection. A crowd quickly formed around the officers. Perry felt someone shake him and groggily came to. He then grabbed the radio handset inside the cruiser and called for an ambulance.

In one brief exchange, Lennie and Suchan had gone from being armed robbers to potential murderers. Canada still had capital punishment in the 1950s, and both men knew there would be little mercy for them if the policemen they shot died. The two Boyd Gang members also knew the police would be searching for the black Monarch. They ditched the car then contacted Camero, ordering her to report it stolen. If police believed her, Camero wouldn't be dragged into what could become a messy murder case.

Back at College and Landsdowne, Detective Tong was being carefully loaded into an ambulance. The emergency vehicle rushed the unconscious officer to Toronto General Hospital. But the prognosis was bad. Even if Tong lived, he would be paralyzed. The bullet had done too much damage to his spine for him to walk again. Detective Perry was also rushed to the hospital. The bullet that had struck him had fractured his arm in several places.

When Mayor Lamport heard of the shootings he was enraged. Declaring that Toronto was suffering from a "reign of terror," he offered a $2000 reward for anyone who provided assistance in tracking down the two shooters.

"We're going to keep Toronto a decent city," Lamport vowed to reporters. "We'll welcome decent citizens, but we don't want the other kind and we're going to make war on them. We're going to catch these fellows and we'll punish them."

Edwin and Dorreen Boyd had been at a movie when Detectives Tong and Perry were shot. When the picture was over, they left the theatre and were stunned to see the headlines in the late-afternoon editions of the papers. While bank robbing seemed almost like a game, shooting cops was definitely not Boyd's style. He would later claim that he could never hate policemen because his father was one.

In response to the shootings, Toronto police launched what they called "the most intensive manhunt in the city's history." Realizing it was a bad idea to stick around Toronto, Lennie and Suchan decided to flee. They travelled by streetcar and bus to Port Credit, a small town outside the city. From there, they hired a taxi to drive them to Oakville. Eventually they made their way to Hamilton, where they rented a hotel room and tried to figure out what to do next.

After thinking it over for a while, the two men stole a car and drove to Montreal. There, Lennie was reunited with Ann Roberts. The two had gotten married a few months earlier, and Ann, who had taken her husband's last name, was pregnant with his child. Together with his new bride, Lennie moved into the single-bedroom apartment he had rented during a previous stay in Montreal.

As Lennie and his wife tried to live like a normal couple, Suchan was on his own and in need of money. Of course, robbing another bank was out of the question. The last thing Suchan wanted to do was draw more attention from the police or the public. Instead of holding up a bank, he decided to sell the Chrysler he had purchased a few months earlier.

Arming himself with a clutch of pistols, Suchan headed out to negotiate with various auto dealers. He kept his guns out of view during these discussions, but was ready to use them if police showed up. In this heavily armed state, Suchan sold his Chrysler to a dealer for $1800. He then took a suitcase out of the car and casually asked the dealer to look after it for him until he could return to collect it.

Little did Suchan know that while he was out negotiating with car dealers, seven Montreal police detectives were paying a visit to his apartment. They had been tipped off by Toronto police, who had tracked down Suchan's Montreal address through a wire transfer that had been sent to him by Anna Camero's mother. Police also had the licence plate and a description of Suchan's Chrysler. When the Montreal enforcements realized that their suspect wasn't at his apartment, the officer in charge of the operation ordered four men to conceal themselves in the residence in case Suchan returned. The three remaining detectives went off in search of Suchan's car.

Suchan ate a lobster dinner at a local restaurant before retiring to his residence. As he walked into his apartment, he spotted the detectives who were waiting for him. Suchan reached for his .455 revolver, the same weapon he had used in the encounter with Detectives

Tong and Perry. But this time, the police reacted first.

Before Suchan could level the .455, an officer raised his own gun and fired. The first shot hit Suchan in the chest. The next one hit him in the stomach. Another round slammed into his arm. The violinist turned gangster was too badly injured to shoot back. The big pistol slipped out of Suchan's hand as he collapsed on the floor. Soon an ambulance arrived and took him, under heavy guard, to Montreal's Queen Elizabeth Hospital.

Montreal police quickly located Suchan's car. More importantly, they recovered the suitcase he had casually left behind with the car dealer. Inside the case were two submachine guns, a pair of revolvers, and hundreds of bullets. Suchan's capture and the police's subsequent findings inspired huge headlines and some typically colourful reporting. "Steve Suchan had a big lobster dinner — as well as two loaded .45s under his belt — when he walked into a police ambush in his posh apartment last night," read the beginning of a story in the *Toronto Telegram*.

After the shootings of Detectives Tong and Perry, and the close call in Suchan's apartment, police were taking no chances. They issued a shoot-to-kill order for Boyd and Lennie. It was no longer a matter of merely arresting the two men, but of killing them if necessary. Both Boyd and Lennie did their best to keep low profiles.

Ambush

Unfortunately for Lennie, a man in his apartment building had sharp eyes. The man was called Henri Cote and he happened to be reading an issue of the *Montreal Gazette* when he came across an article detailing Lennie's involvement with the Boyd Gang. A photo accompanied the article and Cote recognized the person in the picture as the same man who had an apartment near his own. Alarmed, Cote called the police, who were extremely interested in the information he provided.

The day after Cote phoned in his tip, police arrived at Lennie's apartment in force. Lennie and Ann Jackson were inside, oblivious to the fact that a Toronto detective named Jack Gillespie and three officers from the Montreal force were creeping towards their basement suite. Outside the building, a dozen additional officers were in position and awaiting instruction.

By chance, Ann looked out the window and spotted the police. Suddenly very frightened, she warned her husband, who went straight for his guns. An instant later, Detective Gillespie opened the door to Lennie's apartment. The detective instinctively leapt backwards into the hallway as he spotted Lennie inside. Both men began shooting at each other at almost the same time. Lennie missed. Gillespie didn't. Lennie was hit in the abdomen, left arm, and right hand. But even as the heavy slugs slammed into his flesh, Lennie kept on firing. Like an Old West gunfighter who refused to go down, "Tough Lennie" blasted away at police despite his gaping wounds.

Hearing the wild ruckus inside the apartment, the constables standing outside the building began throwing canisters of tear gas through the basement window. When the tear gas wouldn't bring Lennie to his senses, the policemen started firing their machine guns into the apartment. Glass and plaster flew everywhere as bullets slammed through the apartment walls and windows.

Faced with such a ferocious barrage, most criminals would have surrendered immediately. But not Lennie. Even as clouds of tear gas enveloped him and made him weep, he continued to fire away. Lennie had no intention of giving up. His wife, however, had other ideas. Ann was in hysterics, screaming and begging her husband to stop shooting. Lennie just ignored her and kept blasting at police. Somehow, he managed to reload his weapons, even with his injured arm and hand.

"What about the baby!" Ann screamed. "Think about our baby!"

That did the trick. Reminded of the child his wife was carrying, Lennie stopped firing. He turned to Ann and announced that he was giving up. Relieved, Ann left the apartment first, her clothes splattered with blood. She held a pistol in each hand, and dropped both guns on the floor outside the residence. Lennie followed close behind, bleeding profusely from his wounds.

In later years, a legend grew that Lennie used his wife as a human shield, holding her body in front of his as he blazed away at police. Those involved in the Montreal shootout with Lennie denied such a thing ever took place.

Having put an end to the shootout, Lennie Jackson stepped outside his apartment building and surrendered. Because of his injuries, he couldn't raise his hands above his head. He asked if he had hit any constables with his gunfire, and when told that he hadn't, appeared visibly relieved. He was then bundled up and taken to a hospital for emergency treatment.

Meanwhile Boyd was still at large. Back in the boarding house he was staying at in Toronto, Boyd knew it would only be a matter of time before police found him. He was the most wanted criminal in all of Canada. Holed up in his dingy residence, only daring to venture out at night, Boyd took every precaution he could against capture. He never dreamed that a car ad would prove to be his undoing.

Chapter 7
Nabbed

Sergeant of Detectives Adolphus Payne furrowed his brow as he read the classified section of the newspaper. Payne worked on the auto squad of the Toronto police force, and was one of dozens of officers trying to track down the head of the Boyd Gang. But as these other officers were busy tracking down fruitless leads, Payne stayed focussed on the classifieds.

Detective Payne had a long-standing belief that most serious offences usually involved a vehicle. Criminals used vehicles to flee the scene of their crimes, to transport loot, and to scout out new victims. If an officer knew what kind of car or truck a felon used, he or she was that much closer to making an arrest.

After Detective Tong's shooting, Payne had checked provincial records and discovered that Boyd's brother Norman owned a 1949 Austin sedan. The records also indicated that Norman had transferred ownership of the Austin to Dorreen Boyd.

At the time, Dorreen was still living in Pickering, but her children had been packed off to boarding school.

Payne had a hunch that Norman might try to sell his car in order to raise enough cash to pay for a getaway for his sister-in-law and himself. Playing on this hunch, the detective began looking in the classified ads for a '49 Austin sedan. On March 10, 1952, he came across a "For Sale" ad that matched the description of Norman's car. He contacted the number in the ad and pretended to be interested in buying the vehicle. After listening to the voice on the other end of the line, Payne was convinced that he was speaking to Edwin Boyd's brother.

Although Boyd was undoubtedly in hiding some- where, Payne believed that Norman was still in contact with his infamous sibling. The detective was one step closer to nailing Boyd, but he had to work carefully. If police made a move against Norman, it might alert Boyd to the fact that they were on to him. However, if police sat back and did nothing, the head of the Boyd Gang might very well elude them again.

To flush Boyd out of hiding, Detective Payne came up with a devious sting operation. The sting centred on some intricate undercover work by two unlikely operatives. The first was named Harold Jukes, and he worked for the morality squad. Jukes was short and had a baby face, two attributes that would normally stand in the way of a career in the police department. His appearance, however, made him the perfect undercover officer. Because he wasn't tall and tough looking, the criminals he associated with never suspected he was a cop.

While Jukes had a face for undercover work, his partner for this particular sting had a different angle: she wasn't even a cop. Payne selected a department clerk to accompany Jukes. The clerk's name was Patricia Prior, and though largely untrained, this young woman suddenly found herself a key player in a police manhunt. The detective explained his plan to his two new undercover agents. Jukes and Prior would pretend to be a couple looking for a car. They were to contact Norman Boyd and negotiate the sale of his Austin.

The morality squad officer and the department clerk did as they were instructed. They got in touch with Norman and arranged a time to get together at his London Street home. A day later, Jukes and Prior met

Norman, who showed off the Austin. The two undercover officers acted as though they were very interested in purchasing the vehicle. Their mood changed dramatically, however, after Norman explained that he wasn't the actual owner of the car.

Pushing their acting skills to the limit, Jukes and Prior told Norman a longwinded story about how they'd had another car that had been repossessed because the person they purchased it from hadn't been the real owner. They claimed to have received legal advice never to buy another car without getting the registered owner to fill in a release form in front of them.

Norman looked wary, but, wanting to get rid of the Austin, he continued to negotiate with Jukes and Prior. Norman explained that the car belonged to his brother's wife. He would attempt to track her down and get her signature on a written release form. Jukes said that would be fine and provided a phone number where he could be contacted.

Shortly thereafter, Norman called Jukes and told him to be at his house on London Street within a couple hours. Jukes showed up by himself and was given a lien clearance note that contained the signatures of both Norman and Dorreen Boyd. In exchange, Jukes gave Norman a small cash deposit on the '49 Austin, promising he would return a few days later to pay off the balance.

As soon as Jukes had told his superiors about the London Street address, they had put the residence under surveillance. After Jukes left the house, police officers spotted Norman and Dorreen Boyd getting into the '49 Austin sedan. Detective Payne and another officer followed the car in an unmarked cruiser. The Austin drove around the city in a seemingly random pattern. Finally, it ended up in a residential neighbourhood on Heath Street West. As Payne watched, Norman and Dorreen entered a building marked 42 Heath Street. They stayed for half an hour then drove to Spadina Road, where Edwin Boyd's boarding house was located.

Police now had the addresses of several locales where Boyd might be found. Officers began a stakeout of these addresses and quickly hit pay dirt. Boyd was seen getting out of his brother's '49 Austin in front of 42 Heath Street. He had moved out of his Spadina Road digs and planned to stay at Heath Street until an opportune time came to flee the city.

In mid March, Detective Payne, his partner, Detective Ken Craven, and 50 armed officers descended on the Heath Street hideout. They arrived in the middle of the night and cautiously took up positions outside the building. No one wanted to rush in and risk getting shot. Thoughts of the wild gun battle with Lennie Jackson were foremost in everyone's mind. It was assumed that Boyd would be as well-armed as Lennie had been when he shot it out with police in Montreal. Payne waited until dawn before making his move. He crept inside the building and walked gingerly up the stairs to Boyd's apartment. There were three rooms in Boyd's residence, but police had no idea which one he would be in. As far they knew, Boyd might be sitting in his apartment, guns drawn, waiting for police to charge in. It was a thought that made even the toughest cop shiver.

The police could have flushed Boyd out by firing tear gas into the apartment. Or, they could have charged inside all at once and hope to overwhelm him by sheer weight of numbers. Instead, Payne decided that a direct, frontal assault led by one officer — namely himself — would work best. He approached the door to Boyd's apartment then rushed inside, gun in hand. Making his way into the first room of the residence, Payne called Boyd's name. No one was in the first room.

As other police officers came in behind him, Payne continued on to the second room, yelling even louder. Norman Boyd was sleeping on a cot in the corner of the room, but his notorious sibling wasn't there. Finally, the detective made it to the third and final room in the residence, where he found Boyd and Dorreen lying in bed. Norman, Edwin, and Dorreen had been sound asleep and had no idea their hideout was surrounded.

Boyd slowly opened his eyes. The first thing he saw was Payne hovering over him with a gun in his hand. The detective was shouting at him to surrender. Seeing that Payne had the drop on him, Boyd gave himself up without a fight. Other policemen arrived to back Payne up, and soon the small room was packed with law officers. The officers ordered all three Boyds to get dressed, but Dorreen protested this command. Gangster's moll or not, she had no desire to change in a room full of leering policemen. As a compromise, one of the officers gallantly held out a blanket for her to dress behind. He looked away as she put her street clothes on. Once Dorreen and the Boyd brothers were dressed, they were taken into custody.

As police searched Boyd's apartment, they quickly realized they had been dealt a lucky break. Just as authorities had suspected, Boyd was heavily armed. Inside his bedroom, officers found five loaded handguns — two .38 caliber revolvers, a 7.45 mm Beretta automatic pistol, a 9 mm Luger, and a .455 caliber Smith & Wesson revolver. They also found a commando-style knife, ammunition, and a suitcase carrying over $23,000. The pistols in Boyd's bedroom had been positioned so that their handles were pointing upwards, for easy access. If Boyd had been awake when the police had arrived, he could have reached over, grabbed a gun by its handle, and been instantly ready to use it.

Boyd's capture was huge news. Crime-busting Mayor Lamport rushed over to 42 Heath Street as soon as he heard about the arrest. Lamport had been in such a hurry that he forgot to shave for the occasion. The mayor and Toronto police chief John Chisholm posed for press photographers as they examined Boyd's stolen loot.

Reporters had a field day describing the capture. In a typically florid dispatch, the *Toronto Star* had this to say about Boyd's arrest: "The climax of the greatest police manhunt in Canada's crime history was written without a shot today when Edwin Alonzo Boyd, last of a trio of desperate gunmen, looked up from his bed in a Heath St. apartment into the muzzle of a police revolver."

While police celebrated their victory over the Boyd Gang, Detective Tong continued his own battle in the hospital ward. Although he had been hit by just a single bullet, the round had done appalling damage to his strong body. On March 23, 1952, two and a half weeks after he had been shot, Tong died of his injuries. His death was a huge blow to the police department and to the City of Toronto.

A funeral procession for the fallen officer was held

in the east end of Toronto. Police officers lined up shoulder to shoulder along Danforth Avenue as the procession made its way down the street. A police band played funereal airs while officers on horseback looked on, paying respect to a tough, loyal cop. The huge, grim gathering was testament to Tong's popularity on the force. It was also a reminder of the forces of law now arrayed against the Boyd Gang.

Detective Tong's death also came as a jolt to the members of Boyd's gang. It meant that Suchan and Lennie were now facing a murder charge. If the two men were found guilty, they would probably be hung. And a guilty verdict was highly likely; juries and judges had little patience for cop killers.

While he wasn't facing the death penalty, Boyd's future was almost as bleak.

Chapter 8
Reunion Behind Bars

Throughout the spring of 1952, the police dragnet continued to draw tighter. Having captured the Boyd Gang's kingpin, police concentrated on arresting fringe members of the criminal organization. In mid April, Joseph Jackson and his brother-in-law, Allister Gibson, were arrested and charged with armed robbery. A few weeks later, Mary Mitchell was arrested for aiding Boyd after his escape from the Don. Her status as an informer didn't protect her from arrest.

Police also picked up Joseph Lesso, who had returned to Canada following an excursion to Florida that was paid for with Boyd and Willie Jackson's loot. Lesso and his wife Elizabeth were charged with harbouring fugitives from the law.

After his capture, Boyd was taken back to the Don Jail. He was placed in a highly secure part of the prison that consisted of four cells flanked by a corridor. The corridor contained a microphone, put there to monitor Boyd's every sound and move. The microphone was located on the ceiling and was connected to a speaker in the office of Thomas Brand, governor of the prison. Brand was determined to keep Boyd behind bars until his trial. And, since Boyd was the head of a gang that murdered a policeman, guards at the Don were in no mood to make his stay more pleasant. He wasn't even given any reading material, a basic privilege for most prisoners.

Bored, Boyd began practising mental tricks to stimulate his mind and occupy his time. At first, these tricks centred on trying to move matchsticks across his jail cell floor by mind power alone. The results were inconclusive, so Boyd changed his focus. He began trying to mentally impose his will on Governor Brand, directing all his thoughts on trying to change the governor's mind about reading material. To Boyd's great surprise, Governor Brand soon ordered that Boyd be given a Bible and some religious tracts to read.

Flush with the seeming success of his mind control experiments, Boyd continued his attempt to control Governor Brand's thought patterns. If Boyd needed further "proof" that he could influence Brand's mind, it came in the form of a new prisoner in his cellblock. On April 2, 1952, this prisoner was brought in by the guards and deposited in a cell next door to Boyd's. To Boyd's astonishment, his new inmate was none other than Steve Suchan. Having recovered sufficiently from his gunshot wounds, Suchan was healthy enough to serve time in jail until his trial. Though Suchan and Boyd had never been close, they were delighted to see a familiar face.

About a month after Suchan arrived in his cellblock, Boyd got another pleasant surprise. On May 14, Willie Jackson was shipped from the Kingston Penitentiary to the Don Jail to face charges stemming from two hold ups (the Bank of Toronto and the Royal Bank heists). Instead of being placed in a separate wing of the prison, Willie was given a cell near Boyd and Suchan. Boyd's spirits were given a considerable lift. He looked forward to being entertained by Willie.

Ever the amenable type, Willie gladly took part in Boyd's psychic shenanigans. Soon, the two men were praying together. Of course, they weren't praying for world peace or brotherly love, but rather, for God to grant them the means and opportunity to escape. At Willie's suggestion, they also threw in a few prayers to the Devil for good measure. After all, if they were going to pray for an escape, they might as well direct their attention to the king of the underworld.

Their prayers were soon answered. After he had recovered sufficiently from his wounds, Lennie Jackson was transferred into the fourth empty cell in the corridor occupied by Boyd, Willie, and Suchan. Boyd was flabbergasted by this turn of events. The complete Boyd Gang had been reunited behind bars. The four men who had terrorized bank employees across Toronto now occupied the same small patch of prison.

Naturally, Boyd credited this near-miracle to his prayers and his newly developed psychic abilities. He was convinced his attempts to control Governor Brand's mind somehow worked. To Boyd, the only other possibility was that God or the Devil had heard his and Willie's prayers and decided to give them what they wanted.

In retrospect, the governor's decision to put the Boyd Gang together was foolish. After all, Lennie, Willie, and Boyd had already escaped from the Don Jail once before. But at the time, Governor Brand believed he was being perfectly reasonable, even clever. His decision had nothing to do with telepathy or fervent prayers. The way Brand saw it, the men in the Boyd Gang were the most dangerous criminals in Canada, and so it made sense to put them all together in the most secure part of the prison. Even if the men did attempt to escape, Governor Brand was sure the microphone in the corridor would pick up any suspicious discussions or sounds.

Brand was so confident that the men could never break out that he even let the Boyd Gang leave their cells during the daytime. The four prisoners were now able to stroll up and down the corridor that lined their cellblock. Governor Brand also supplied the men with a table, benches, and some playing cards.

Boyd was elated. He had gone from being alone in his cell with no reading material, to having his old criminal comrades around to keep him company. He could leave his cell during the day, eat at a table with his confederates, and play cards to help pass the time. Boyd and the rest of his gang returned the governor's consideration by plotting a new escape.

Willie Jackson took the lead in setting the men's second escape plan in motion. Just as Harold Jukes made a great undercover officer because he didn't look like a cop, Willie was the perfect point man to plan an escape. All the guards thought he was a genial dunce who wasn't capable of the kind of trickery involved in plotting a jailbreak.

However, in between cracking jokes and doing routines, Willie managed to secure a tiny piece of flat steel, along with a file. Willie later claimed he received these items from his lawyer during a meeting at the prison.

The Boyd Gang hoped to make a replica of the cell key by filing the piece of flat steel. A key would allow them to leave their cells at will. While governor Brand let the men to mingle in the corridor during the day, he wasn't foolish enough to let them out of their cells at night. It was decided that Boyd would do the actual filing. The problem, of course, was that he had no idea how the key had been cut. So Willie took it upon himself to find out.

One evening, Willie approached the guard who was locking the Boyd Gang members in their cells. In his usual clownish manner, Willie asked if he could lock Suchan's cell. He grabbed at the key in the guard's hand and squeezed it tight. Letting go a moment later, Willie grinned at the guard, who thought nothing of the incident. The guard figured the inmate was just goofing around, as usual. In actuality, Willie had grabbed at the key with a very serious scheme in mind. By holding it tight in his hand, he had managed to imprint the shape of the key on his palm. After going back to his cell, Willie held out his palm and drew the outline of the key on the wall. His crude sketch gave Boyd a crucial blueprint from which to work.

To cover up the sound of Boyd's filing, the men sang, flushed the toilet frequently, and engaged in contrived arguments. If Governor Brand heard anything unusual as he listened in, he didn't do anything about it. Boyd hid the piece of steel and the file by the base of his toilet. This was an area that guards tended not to search carefully.

While his cellblock mates provided cover, Boyd filed the flat piece of steel until its ridges and grooves resembled that of the cell-door key. When the replica key was finished, the Boyd Gang were able to let themselves out of their cells at will. Now all they needed was a hacksaw blade to cut through the double bars on the window in their corridor. Once again, Willie came through for the gang. He secured a hacksaw blade with the alleged help of his lawyer.

As the days passed, the Boyd Gang established a new routine. Around dawn, they would open their cells with the homemade key. Then, Willie or Boyd would use the hacksaw to cut through the bars on the window in the corridor. Just as they had done in their first escape, the men disguised the cuts in the bars with a mixture of dirt and soap.

The bank robbers only worked on the bars for a few minutes at a time. They sawed every morning at around

5:30, when there were usually no guards patrolling the area. To block any unusual sounds that might be picked up in Governor Brand's office, the gang moved their table underneath the microphone in the corridor ceiling. They then took turns standing on the table, holding a pillow over the screen in front of the microphone. When the men weren't using the hacksaw, they hid it in a crack in the wooden floor.

For their first escape, the Boyd Gang had only needed to saw through one window bar. Now, because the window in their cellblock had double bars, they had to cut through two. Slowly and systematically, Boyd and Willie sawed through both bars, always careful to hide their progress with soap and dirt.

By late August of 1952, about five months after Boyd's arrest, the two bars had been completely sliced through. Early one morning, the Boyd Gang removed the bars from the window and prepared to escape. As he was the smallest of the four, Boyd tried the window first. He could only get his head and shoulders through the opening. Suchan and the two Jacksons watched with mounting dismay. If Boyd couldn't make it out, chances were slim that anyone else could. Boyd got down from the window and let Willie see if he could get through the opening. No dice. The Boyd Gang would have to saw through two more bars if they wanted to escape.

The men gingerly replaced the two sawed bars in the window. They slapped soap and dirt over the cuts, but fretted that the slightest breeze — or a guard's touch — might knock the bars down. Fortunately, the guards didn't seem to notice that anything was amiss. The bars stayed in place, which allowed the Boyd Gang to continue their early-morning labours.

Finally, on a morning in early September, the men were ready to make a break for freedom. Before leaving his cell, Lennie fit an enamel drinking cup over his stump. Police had confiscated his artificial foot, so he had to make do. Shortly before daybreak, the Boyd Gang removed the four sawed bars from the window and climbed through. Suchan barely fit, but eventually they all made it out the opening.

As the men cautiously crawled out along a wall, they spotted a policeman patrolling the grounds below. The whole gang froze. They had timed the comings and goings of all the guards, but hadn't expected to see a cop patrolling near the jail. If the constable looked up, he would certainly spot the four escaped prisoners in the early morning light.

After a few heart-pounding minutes, the patrolman disappeared inside a building. The Boyd Gang issued a collective sigh of relief then moved to the edge of the wall. One by one, they jumped to the ground. It was nearly a 16-foot drop, but the four men landed with few problems. Lennie's enamel cup had fallen off as he'd positioned himself to jump, but he still got to the ground without difficulty. Willie then retrieved the cup for him and Lennie put it back in place on his stump.

The men had done it. Thanks in large part to Willie's initiative, they had successfully escaped from the Don Jail for a second time. It was an impressive achievement, and it was made that much sweeter by the fact that they had been held in a supposedly escape-proof part of the prison.

Of course, the Boyd Gang had no time to pat themselves on the back. The sun was coming up and it would only be a matter of minutes before someone noticed they were gone. The men quickly headed towards the nearby Don Valley, a place they were familiar with from their previous jailbreak. Before anyone at the prison could sound an alarm, the gang had disappeared into the valley's thicket of trees, bushes, and tall grass.

Chapter 9
Manhunt

At around 7 A.M. on the morning of the escape, guards at the Don Jail finally noticed the Boyd Gang was gone. Governor Brand was alerted and within minutes, the jail was swarming with guards and police. Authorities combed the prison and its grounds looking for any sign of Boyd, Suchan, and the two Jacksons. They were joined by firefighters, who used their extension ladders to inspect the roof of the prison in the hopes of finding the four men hiding there.

Newspaper reporters and other journalists started to arrive at the jail as police slowly pieced together the details of the Boyd Gang's escape. By this time, the gang members were making their way up the Don Valley. They planned on heading north to hide out in an abandoned farm in the North York area until they could find a way out of Toronto.

In 1952, the Don Valley was largely undeveloped. There was no expressway running through it, as there is today, and the area consisted largely of brush. This heavy brush made the going tough. Lacking proper hiking equipment or strong boots, the Boyd Gang had to work their way through the dense shrubs by hand. To make matters worse, the men were clad only in their prison-issue uniforms, which didn't do much to keep out the autumn chill.

Lennie had a particularly hard time. Not only did he lack a proper prosthetic foot, he also suffered from asthma and allergies. As the gang made their way north, Lennie was finding it increasingly difficult to breath. But being the tough guy that he was, he kept moving, gasping for breath as he followed the others.

While it was difficult to navigate, the Don Valley was an excellent choice for an escape route. The same dense underbrush that impeded the gang's progress served to hide them from view. An airplane or helicopter flying overhead would have difficulty seeing the men, even if they were directly below. The valley would also be a challenge for policemen who were chasing the gang on foot or by car.

* * *

The Boyd Gang's second escape from the Don Jail triggered an enormous reaction from the public, the press, and politicians. Mayor Lamport, who had been cottaging at Lake Simcoe when the jailbreak occurred, was furious when he heard the news. He rushed back to Toronto and gave several angry interviews to reporters. "Who in blazes was such a fool to put them in one cell block?" demanded Lamport. "The men were allowed to eat together, sleep together and were practically given club car privileges ... It's pretty shabby treatment for our police who have done all they can and are let down like this."

As the mayor aired his anger, the local papers published story after story on the escape. "Boyd, Killer Pals on Loose," read the headline in the *Toronto Telegram*, "Police Shoot on Sight". In the *Toronto Star*, Jocko Thomas wrote the following: "Edwin Alonzo Boyd, master bank robber, and three members of his gang, regarded as the most desperate criminals ever locked in the Don Jail, have sawed their way out and every policeman in Ontario was alerted for the hunt today, with orders of shoot to kill."

The City of Toronto and the Canadian Bankers Association quickly put together a reward for the recapture of the Boyd Gang. This reward came to the hefty sum of $26,000. The first time the Boyd Gang had escaped from the Don, the reward had been set at $500. The men had come a long way in the eyes of the law.

Ontario premier Leslie Frost even got in on the act. He announced that he would convene a royal commission to look into the escape.

Speculation was rife that the Boyd Gang had disappeared to an obscure corner of Canada. The gang was "sighted" in cities across the country. Pundits made wild predictions about what the gang would do next.

"The Edwin Boyd Gang had active plans ... and may still have these plans ... to stick up two, three or even four banks at the same time in the Toronto district. They told me this themselves," wrote Gordon Sinclair in the *Toronto Star*.

In reality, the Boyd Gang was far more interested in making tracks up the Don Valley and finding a hideout than they were in robbing banks. Eventually, the four men came to an abandoned property called the Doner Farm. The farm contained an empty house and barn. Upon examining both, the gang decided to stay in the barn. It was cleaner than the house, which was filled with dirt and debris.

Boyd, Suchan, Lennie, and Willie settled into their new digs. Their plan was to sleep in the barn at night and hide in the woods during the day. They figured that if they stayed in the woods all day, it would be less likely that someone would spot them.

For Boyd, the second jailbreak marked an anniversary of sorts. It came nearly three years to the day that he had committed his first bank robbery. In that period of time, he had gone from being a drunken stick-up man to one of the most infamous criminals in the country. As he bunked down in the barn, it's doubtful that Boyd felt like celebrating this singular achievement.

After they'd settled in at the Doner Farm, Suchan left his comrades for an evening. When he returned, he was carrying clothes, an artificial foot for Lennie, and three pistols — gifts from Suchan's underworld associates.

As the Boyd Gang continued to hide out, the press and public were becoming hysterical about the jailbreak. The local papers put the escape on their front pages day after day, even when there was no news to report. Meanwhile, a total of 2000 policemen were enlisted in the search for the gang. Officers expected trouble if they caught up with the four men, and were ready to shoot it out if necessary.

Despite their celebrity status, Boyd, Suchan, and the two Jacksons were living like peasants at the Doner

Farm. The property was isolated, and the men had virtually no food. They took to scrounging potatoes, apples, and carrots from nearby farms. At one point, desperate to eat something besides dirty fruit and vegetables, the gang disguised Willie and sent him out on a shopping expedition. Willie cautiously made his way to a nearby plaza. In his pockets, he carried the small amount of cash the four men had taken with them during their jailbreak. Pleased that no one seemed to recognize him, Willie purchased beans, cold cuts, bread, cheese, and other staples. He also took the time to read several newspaper headlines that featured updates on the Boyd Gang's escape.

When he was done his errands, Willie strolled back to the barn, where his hungry comrades greeted him like a returning hero. They eagerly consumed the food Willie bought, and for a few minutes, were able to forget the fact that thousands of cops were on their trail.

On September 11, 1952, all three major Toronto newspapers ran a heartfelt plea from Dorreen Boyd. "My Dearest Eddie," wrote Dorreen, "Am I asking too much of you under the circumstances to give yourself up? If to anyone, to me, or to the men both you and I know would give you a fair deal. I have thought this over so much in the past three days, and knowing me as your devoted wife, I'll wait for you no matter what the outcome may be. God willing, we will have the privilege of growing old together. This is all I ask of you, and remember always I love you."

Boyd probably didn't see the letter, and if he did, it failed to persuade him. The Boyd Gang might have been living rough at the Doner Farm, but they weren't eager to give themselves up. Even Lennie, who was suffering terribly with his allergies, had no intention of surrendering.

But despite all their precautions and attempts to keep a low profile, the Boyd Gang was spotted at the Doner Farm. Local farmers and workmen tipped the North York police about a group of tramps who seemed to be living on the property. On September 16, a pair of policemen decided to check out the Doner place to see if these tips were valid. The constables weren't really expecting to come across the Boyd Gang.

The road leading into the Doner Farm was being torn up by work crews and was packed with construction equipment. This meant the police had to park their cruiser some distance away and approach the farm on foot. As they walked into the barn, the two officers almost literally stumbled across Boyd, Willy, and Lennie. The convicts were caught totally by surprise. Either they had forgotten to post a sentry or someone had gotten sloppy.

Though the three Boyd Gang members had weapons inside the barn, they didn't try to use them. Just as Boyd had given up without a struggle when he woke up to find Detective Payne pointing a gun at him, the men surrendered peacefully to the two astonished police officers. The arrest had been a happy accident; because the constables were walking, not driving, the Boyd Gang members in the barn hadn't heard their approach. Had the police driven up in a cruiser, they would have given their presence away and their reception would undoubtedly have been much different.

According to Jocko Thomas of the *Toronto Star*, Steve Suchan — who had been out gathering apples when the rest of the gang was arrested — didn't give up so easily. "Three constables were sent to search the barn for firearms," wrote Jocko in his memoirs. "Only luck saved them from suffering the same fate as Detective Tong. As they walked in, they heard a clicking sound in the hayloft. They looked up and found themselves looking at Steve Suchan and the muzzle of an automatic pistol."

Jocko Thomas went on to write that "[Suchan] was trying very hard to kill them, but his gun had jammed ... even as the three constables watched, Suchan tried a couple more times to get a shot off, then the cops had him covered. Suchan disgustedly threw the jammed pistol into the hay."

Norman Boyd, left, Edwin Boyd, centre, and Willie Jackson
are escorted from a police vehicle in October 1952

As colourful as this description was, it simply
wasn't true. Suchan did have a gun in his belt, but he
made no attempt to use it. When he returned to the
barn, pail of apples in hand, police were waiting for him.

They told him to give up and he did. Suchan was quickly handcuffed and transported to a secure lockup.

With Suchan's arrest, the Boyd Gang saga had come to a close. Now that all the key members were back in custody, police vowed the gang would never escape again. There was only one way the Boyd Gang could walk as free men: by being acquitted in court. And the odds of that happening were about the same as Edwin Alonzo Boyd being hired as a bank manager.

Chapter 10
Trials and Tribulations

Following their arrest, Boyd, Willie, Lennie, and Suchan were taken to the North York police station. The place was a madhouse. There were dozens of reporters and hundreds of curious spectators all vying for a view of the infamous Boyd Gang. Mayor Lamport raced to the police station to get his picture taken, as did Toronto police chief John Chisholm. The mayor took the time to berate the Boyd Gang for their criminal lifestyle and enthusiasm for jailbreaks.

"You can't beat society this way," scolded Lamport, as reporters nearby wrote down every word. The mayor said he was happy enough to cry. The Boyd Gang's escapades and the city's inability to keep them behind bars had been a huge embarrassment for law officials. That evening, Lamport described the gang as "a bunch of whipped lambs."

But whipped or not, the prisoners seemed surprisingly upbeat at the North York police station. They joked around with reporters and mugged for the cameras. The papers of course, played up the capture to the hilt. "Nab Boyd Gang" read an enormous headline in the *Globe and Mail*. A subhead to the story read, "Cringe Before 2 Detectives."

During interviews with reporters, Boyd made a flippant comment about being prepared to escape once more. The *Toronto Star* featured this remark in a front-page headline that read "I'll Saw My Way Out Again." Boyd also told a reporter to keep his car filled with gas, so he could use it in another jailbreak.

The Boyd Gang were eventually brought back to the Don Jail. They were placed in their old cellblock, but there was no way they could escape again. New, super tough steel bars had been placed on the windows near their cells. In addition, a squad of seven Ontario Provincial Police officers were put in charge of guarding the men around the clock. This marked the first time in the Don Jail's history that police were used for day and night guard duty.

The trials of all the members of the Boyd Gang began on September 22, 1952 in the courtrooms of Old City Hall in Toronto. Security was very tight. Toronto police put a special guard detail on the Don Jail to ensure the Boyd Gang didn't escape for a third time. Police stood in a ring around the prison each evening while the trials were on.

The trials were short, lasting only three weeks. In the end, the Boyd Gang drew guilty verdicts all around. Willie Jackson was given 20 years concurrent for two armed robberies plus time for two escapes. Photos of Willie showed him being led from the courtroom with a cigar in his mouth. He used the stogie as a prop, moving it around his mouth as he smirked at the cameras.

Joseph and Elizabeth Lesso were found guilty of harbouring fugitives and received nine months and six months, respectively. Mary Mitchell was given six months for harbouring fugitives, while fringe Boyd Gang member Allister Gibson drew eight years. Norman Boyd got three years for armed robbery while Willie's brother, Joseph Jackson, was given 10 years.

Suchan and Lennie were tried separately for the murder of Detective Eddie Tong. Their trial began on September 22 and only lasted a short time. Both Lennie and Suchan claimed that they didn't know the car that pulled up to them at the intersection was a police cruiser. Lennie said he was familiar with Detective Tong, but wasn't aware he was the man who had been shot during the altercation. Suchan admitted he fired shots in the general direction of Tong and Perry's cruiser, but claimed he was just trying to knock out the engine.

On December 16, 1952, as opponents of the death penalty marched outside, Steve Suchan and Lennie Jackson were hung at the Don Jail. They were among the last criminals to be put to death in Canada, where capital punishment would soon be abolished.

As for Edwin Boyd, the head of Canada's most notorious gang of criminals managed to escape the hangman. The judge handed Boyd eight life terms for robbing banks and stealing cars. In passing judgment, the court made it clear that they thought Boyd was a big enough threat to keep him locked up for the rest of his life.

Epilogue

Following his trial, Boyd was taken to Kingston Penitentiary to serve out his sentence.

In spite of his celebrity status, Boyd went out of his way to maintain a low profile in the prison. He spent much of his time reading and kept largely to himself. Boyd even became interested in religion and began studying various spiritual tomes. But this time around, Boyd didn't pray to God or the Devil to help him escape. He showed no interest in pursuing his psychic mind games, but concentrated instead on improving his life.

Of course, this isn't to say that Boyd was particularly happy at Kingston. He continued to harbour a desire to escape. In 1954, guards found parts of a hacksaw blade in Boyd's cell. As a result, he was placed in solitary confinement and never did manage to successfully break out of jail a third time.

But if Boyd couldn't break out of prison, he was determined to charm his way out. He set about convincing those around him that he was reformed. Outside the jail, Dorreen Boyd pled her husband's case to legal authorities and newspaper reporters. Some of them were sympathetic and put in a good word for Boyd.

In 1962, Edwin Boyd was granted parole. A few months after his release, Boyd formed a relationship with a teenage girl. While Boyd insisted the relationship was entirely platonic, the unusual friendship went against his parole conditions and he soon found himself back behind bars. Boyd stayed in prison until 1966, when he was paroled once again. This time he stayed out of jail for good. His total sentence, which amounted to 12 years behind bars, had been considerably shorter than eight life terms.

Once Boyd was released, his main concern was to stay out of the public spotlight. Authorities granted his request. He was given a new name and travelled to British Columbia to start life anew. He landed a job driving a van for handicapped adults and fell in love with a woman he met on the van. Boyd married her in 1970, after divorcing Dorreen.

While living in British Columbia, Boyd occasionally hung out with Willie Jackson, who had also been released from prison in the 1960s. Willie took a job as a janitor and spent his remaining years mopping floors and getting drunk.

In the mid 1970s, Boyd moved into a special home designed to accommodate his wife, who got around in a wheelchair. Not long after the couple had settled in, another woman in a wheelchair — a friend of Boyd's wife's — moved into the home as well. Boyd looked after both ladies and earned a reputation as a kind, helpful man.

Of course, the legend of the Boyd Gang never died. Books, movies, and television shows created after Boyd's release from jail all drew attention to his brief but colourful criminal career. In the late 1990s, the Canadian Broadcasting Corporation (CBC) interviewed Boyd for a "Life and Times" documentary. The show featured ample commentary by the white-haired Boyd. He came across as a redeemed scoundrel who was spending his remaining years helping his handicapped wife. The CBC program, and other news stories published in Boyd's later life, served to reinforce his image as a "gentleman bank robber."

The question, of course, was whether the "Boyd Legend" was true or not. In his CBC interview, Boyd himself admitted that he "did a few things that could have got [him] hung," and hinted that he had committed crimes for which he was never caught. A CBC follow-up documentary, aired in late 2002, centred on one very specific crime for which Boyd was never charged.

The crime involved the double murder of a man and woman, found stuffed in the trunk of a Chevy coupe in Toronto's High Park. This felony had been committed in September of 1947, but had never been solved. For decades, the High Park murder case remained a mystery. The CBC follow-up documentary named a suspect in the long-unsolved crime: Edwin Boyd.

Far from buying into the image of Boyd as a Jesse James-like folk hero, this CBC documentary painted Boyd as a greedy psychopath and alleged killer. The CBC admitted that Boyd had no obvious motive for the crime and that their evidence was circumstantial. Nonetheless, by combining Boyd's deathbed commentary with an analysis of his movements in the period the crime was committed, the CBC was sure they had their man.

Boyd himself had no comment. He died peacefully a few months before the documentary aired, gentleman image intact. He was 88 years old, and still the most famous bank robber Canada had ever produced.

About the Author

Nate Hendley is a freelance writer who lives in Toronto.